Witness Awakening

FINDING PEACE AND HEALING IN THE MIDST OF CHILDHOOD TRAUMA

MARIE MCCARTHY

Publishing services provided by 

Disclaimer: The guidance in this book is not intended to be a substitute for the medical or mental health advice of a licensed physician. The reader should consult with their doctor in any matters relating to his/her health.

ISBN-13: 978-1-9860-3909-3

ISBN-10: 1986039099

This book is dedicated to survivors of childhood trauma seeking inner peace, and those supporting them.

Contents

Acknowledgments

Giving Thanks

I want to give thanks to God, who has loved and supported me every single moment, even when I was unaware of Divine presence. I also want to give thanks to my husband for all his support and love throughout our journey together. He is a beautiful gift, and I love him with all my heart. Thank you to my precious children, who loved and accepted me through difficult times. I want to thank my professional helpers Georgette Kelly (deceased, Jungian psychoanalyst), Patti Packard (sexual assault therapist), and Angela Dumas (spiritual health coach). Thank you also to my mother, my sisters, my cousin Jim, and my friends. And finally, thanks to Marianne Williamson for her insightful, inspiring, and loving books, which comforted me and continue to help move my healing forward.

Author's Note

To My Sister and Brother Survivors

Childhood trauma, especially repeated abuse, creates soul-crushing wounds. Can you relate to the daily struggles of managing symptoms from childhood trauma, like feeling overwhelmed, scared, and—at times—tormented? Sadly, as survivors we have suffered at the hands of others. Many of us are plagued by chronic physical and mental illness because we have been unable to heal. *We do not have to stay in that place*, being stuck in our woundedness, because at our core we are spiritual beings with tremendous potential to heal. The gift of peace and thriving, versus just surviving, is actually attainable. There are many documented success stories of people just like you and me who have made that transformation. You and I have the same potential. Our darkest moments can be transformed into our strongest and most passionate parts.

Thank you for choosing to join me on my personal journey toward wholeness. In the following pages, I will describe self-awareness work that helped me with getting to my other side. I'm hoping I can support you by sharing my recovery story—I pray it inspires you to continue moving forward with your own healing. By sticking together and telling our truth as survivors, we are stronger as a group. We can witness ourselves and each other transforming from feeling small and scared, to feeling strong and empowered. You can be a witness to your trauma self and awaken to your gift of peace.

While working through my inner darkness as an adult, I needed to know I wasn't the only one going through this hell, that I wasn't alone with my pain or the way it was being expressed. We as survivors aren't insane; rather, we're suffering from trauma injuries. I'm holding the intention that you remember there is hope of coming out on the other side. The other side doesn't have to be total symptom cessation. For most of us, recovery is learning how to connect with ourselves and more successfully manage the enormous damage that our childhood trauma caused.

As you read my story, you may feel that what I needed to do to recover is too much and took too long. I hope you will consider that every person's journey is different, and mine was as it needed to be; it helped me heal and prepared me to be the best trauma recovery therapist I can be. I believe that if I could have remembered at an earlier age, my healing would have moved along much faster.

No matter how fearful or hopeless facing the darkness inside may seem, it won't kill us. What can kill us is spending our whole life self-medicating by feeding addictions and running away from our pain and ultimately, from the truth. Living with this inner torment will likely lead to chronic illness and possibly suicide. Healing from trauma is an intense journey, and it requires loving helpers and supportive survivors to guide us through our process until we can stand strong on our own.

With love and hope for your healing,
Marie

Your Free Guided Meditation for Relaxation

Before you begin reading this book, I have a free bonus to offer you.

In addition to the information already provided in this book, I have created a guided meditation that can assist you with relaxation and sleep. Every time you listen, you will strengthen your association with hearing the meditation and becoming more relaxed which can assist you when you're anxious or can't find the off switch for your thoughts.

To receive your free guided meditation, sign up for the my mailing list by visiting:

www.witnessawakening.com/witnessawakeningbook

Signing up will also notify you of any pending book releases or updated content. By subscribing you will be first in line for exclusive deals and future book giveaways.

Immediately after signing up you'll be sent an email with access to the bonus.

Peaceful Blessings,

–Marie McCarthy

Protective Tools

I'm imagining telling you my story over a cup of tea. But before I start, I'd like to share some tools you might use to protect yourself, to avoid activating your trauma. I've left out disturbing information that I believed might be highly triggering. My purpose is to describe my journey of healing, not to trigger your own trauma; however, I need to share enough detail for you to understand what happened and how it played out. In an effort to support you as a survivor, or anyone who may find certain sections of my story difficult to read, I offer the following information about triggers and protective tools.

A *trigger* is anything that reminds a person of his or her trauma and causes uncharacteristic and exaggerated responses to life situations. An example might be sudden feelings of intense fear, being "spaced-out," or feeling childlike in response to something that wouldn't normally warrant that reaction. While triggers may be debilitating and take some time to recover from, they can also act as a positive catalyst to move you forward on your journey. They have the ability to aid you in realizing that something happened to you and that it needs to be addressed.

Understanding and setting *boundaries* to protect ourselves is also important. My boundaries were trampled on by abusers when I was little. Their invasions disabled my boundary system until I didn't know that boundaries even existed or that I had a right to set a boundary by saying no to protect myself. Before I knew about boundaries, other people's emotions would affect me to the point that I felt revictimized. I needed to learn how to protect myself by reminding myself that others' "stuff" was not mine and I shouldn't take their stuff on as my own. Setting boundaries is a big deal for sexual assault survivors. It's extremely important to keep the boundaries of where *you* start and *others* begin, as clear as possible.

If you're getting triggered or chaotic, remember that you have the power to help yourself with protective tools. For example, if I feel myself getting negatively emotionally charged or triggered, I first evaluate what is happening and determine if I'm able to either remove the trigger, or remove myself from the situation. I make a conscious decision about whether or not I want or need to be exposed to something. Next, I ground myself in the present moment by reminding myself, "I'm an adult now, and I'm safe." I tell myself, "**SHIELDS UP**," as a reminder that I can protect myself by putting up a boundary. That boundary can be a physical one like walking away, or it can be imaginary. A wonderful tool offered to me by my sexual assault counselor involves visualizing myself standing safely in the center of a corral with a fence around the perimeter. Everything is outside that perimeter, and nothing can touch or affect me. If I sense that my exposure will be intense, I go further and imagine myself going into an army tank or full body armor like a knight.

In the following chapters, the **SHIELDS UP** term will be a reminder for you to consciously protect yourself as I'm about to discuss something disturbing. This will allow you to check in with yourself and decide if you want to continue reading and, if so, psychologically protect yourself using boundary tools. The phrase "**DEEP**

BREATH" will let you know I'm done talking about the potentially disturbing section. In an effort to help you with the more highly triggering parts of my story, I've placed most of the trauma events in the first chapter to prevent them from coming up over and over. My story begins in the third person to show you one of the tools I use to make telling my trauma events more bearable.

The Unprotected Child

Childhood Traumas

There was a little girl who appeared to be the ideal healthy and loving child. She reminded me of a beautiful lotus flower, its velvety white petals innocently stretched out to the world. However, the rest of her petals were hidden in a clenched chaotic mass, holding secrets.

Her name was Marie, and she was born into a middle-class white family in the early sixties to parents whose marriage was struggling. Her parents' strained marriage pushed her mother to contemplate drowning herself while she was pregnant with Marie. It was an odd choice, since her mother would normally turn white at the thought of going into the water. Sadly, depression had set in for the mother-to-be.

Following Marie's birth, her father left, and she—along with her mother and two older sisters, eight and three years old—lived in a motel for a bit. Her mother only touched her when she had to do basic care, such as propping up Marie's bottle or changing her soiled diaper. There probably weren't moments of staring into her big baby eyes, cherishing her and cuddling with her. Since Marie's mother was distressed, she found it easier to complete tasks than to connect emotionally with her children. Not long after the family moved into the motel, Marie was sent to live with her grandparents; she bonded with them as if they were her mom and dad. Her biological parents did get back together for thirteen more years, so Marie moved back in with them.

Marie grew into a cute freckle-faced girl with Irish looks; she had big brown eyes and a warm, loving smile. She was always busy doing something—taking trips to the frog pond, riding her bicycle, and playing with her Barbie dolls were just a few of her passions. Her trips to the frog pond at five years old were an adventure down a heavily wooded road at her summer home. She spent hours lifting up lily pads to search for salamanders, frogs, and tadpoles. Rarely was anyone there. Marie would immerse herself in fantasy while running with iridescent fireflies and smelling the sweet yet unpleasant combination of standing water and wildflowers. She loved people and animals, and she had a wonderful ability to make friends.

More than anything, Marie craved the warm company of loving adults, and she would seek out elders at her summer home, where she felt at the center of their attention. One couple would invite her in and light up with joy at the sight of her. At each visit, the man would take her to the basement to pick out her favorite flavor of soda. He would then light a fire in the fireplace upstairs and throw crystals into it that made the fire light up with colors. The woman was a retired teacher and would help Marie with her alphabet, since she recognized a learning difficulty as Marie was approaching six years old.

There was another elderly couple down the road. The woman first caught Marie's eye when she rode down the street in what looked like an adult-sized tricycle with a big basket. *Wow*, Marie thought, *she must be special to have a bike like that!* Visits would consist of the couple and Marie sitting in their living room talking. The couple would offer her mushy chocolate chip cookies and a soda, which made Marie's day! Thank God the elderly couples were good people!

Marie's father was successful in his career, which provided many opportunities, like having a second home, going horseback riding, sailing, and playing tennis. Marie loved her dad very much, but he was a workaholic and wasn't around that much. The parenting role was solely placed in her mother's lap. Marie's life *appeared* just right, with her nice clothes, great vacations, and her tall and strikingly beautiful stay-at-home mother.

However, within her existed a deep, dark well of pain, though she didn't know why until many years later in her forties, when she started remembering traumatic events. What follows is one of her remembering experiences.

I'm guessing you already figured out that Little Marie is me.

* * *

I'm driving down an unpaved back road and feeling emotionally shaky. The woman on the phone is giving me an ultimatum: "Either you do what I say, or I won't sponsor you." My emotional state quickly escalates, and I'm feeling raw—not at all like a forty-three-year-old woman but like a helpless child who's being threatened and overcome by a tidal wave of terror. My whole body starts shaking violently. I hang up the phone, drop it, and pull over. *What's happening? Oh my God! Where are these horrible childlike sounds coming from? Is that me?*

I am yelling, gagging, sobbing, and flailing about, contorting my body in my car as if I'm being attacked. I'm hearing disturbing sounds of pain and struggle. I want to throw up. I gag until I spit up some blood. It feels like something is being released from my body, as if my body is physically letting something out. Now I feel robotic and detached from my body. I was fighting someone or something with emotional and physical memories, but now I'm limp. I think I'm experiencing an event, but I can't see anything in my mind.

This is awful—so awful. Slowly the terror begins to pass, and I feel like I'm in a dream now. As I make my way home, I don't think it's safe for me to drive in this detached state. What is going on?

After returning home, I tell my husband something really upsetting happened to me in the car, but I don't know what it was. I am completely confused. All I can think of is, *What the hell was that?* I can't control my body in the way I'm used to; I am exhausted, scared, sad, and angry. But at who? At what? My body feels beaten up. The enormous stress that my heart, nervous system, and muscles experienced is worrisome. It feels like my teeth will cave in from the force of my clenching, and afterward my jaw is in pain.

* * *

Not long after this experience, I shared this with someone at a women's group who said, "Marie, it sounds like you had a flashback." Days later, as I meditated on my prayer mat, I recalled and then journaled the following visual memories associated with the flashback in my car:

(SHIELDS UP) Some of the details remain blurry, and I only have memory fragments, but the memory that was clear was that I'm about four years old.

> *I feel a man stuffing something attached to him into my little mouth. I'm gagging and feel as though my jaw is being split open. My body wants to vomit but can't. I'm in pain, and I think to myself, What's happening? I'm being pushed down, and I can't escape. I'm trying to get away but can't. Why is this man being so mean to me? What is he doing? I'm so scared! Then suddenly, I'm limp, and I don't think I'm in my body anymore. I see a child on the floor, looking dead with blank eyes. That's me! I'm not moving. I see the man, too, and he notices me looking dead. He's scared at how lifeless I look. He leaves me lying here.*

As I came out of my memory, I felt surreal. I experienced an odd, robotic feeling as if my body were a machine that I was having trouble controlling. Everything moved in slow motion. A thought to *get up* was so far removed from my ability to respond that it took time for my mind to make a connection with my body and then move. I felt confused and unsure of what was happening. **(DEEP BREATH)**

Can you imagine what kind of a monster one must be to assault a sweet little girl like this?

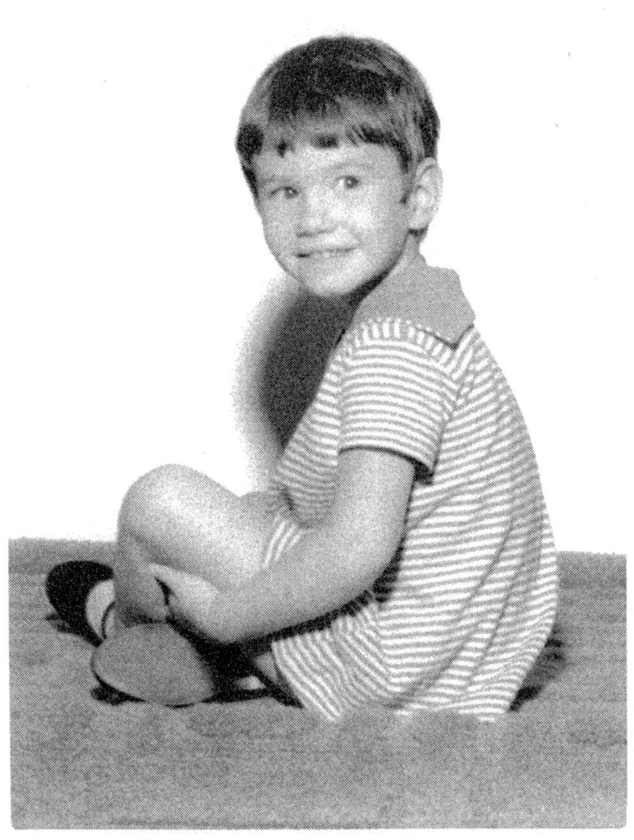

After the flashback, I realized I'd had a traumatic, life-changing experience at the age of four. Thirty-nine years later, at forty-three years old, the images came to me so vividly that *I actually felt I was four years old* and was experiencing a rape. During the assault, I had dissociated to the point of leaving my body altogether, and it was at this point that I repressed all memory of what had happened. The limp, dead-looking period is called the *immobility or collapsing trauma*

state, and a rigid posture would be a *freeze trauma state*; these can occur when a person feels that his or her life is threatened.

Soon after this flashback, I remembered a recurring nightmare I had dreamed many times throughout my childhood:

> *I'm in my yard and hear a roaring, rumbling sound. Terror grips every muscle and nerve in my body as I tense up like a stone statue. I don't want to look, it's too scary! I slowly turn toward the sound. Oh my God! It's water—a gigantic wave or wall of water, and it's coming right at me. I rise above it, out of my body, and watch it annihilate my world: every tree, house, person, and animal—all gone. Sheer terror radiates through me.*

When I remembered that dream from my childhood, I sensed that it had begun after the sexual assault described above. I think it symbolized the tidal wave of repressed trauma memories and emotions secretly stored under the surface of my consciousness. It also spoke to the insidious nature of trauma and its aftereffects, knowing on some level that my world of trust and innocence had been permanently soiled.

My mother had no idea I was being sexually assaulted. She thought her little girl was safe at a neighbor's house, and I never remembered it nor spoke of it until I had the flashback so many years after the attack. We moved not long after the incident, and I can't recall the man's face or name.

* * *

Was this the last flashback, or was I going to have more? What awful things may be hidden within my mind? This really made me question what else I had forgotten. Unfortunately, a month later, I had a foreboding feeling that something was coming up. I was taking a break in a warm bath, and a life-changing memory began.

(SHIELDS UP) *I'm nine or ten years old. On this awful day, I've just come home from school, and the house is empty. I hear a knock at the door and open it. A man is forcing his way in, and his eyes are violent and angry. I feel terror in the air as the hair on the back of my neck stands up. Oh no, he's charging at me. He forces me onto the staircase right by the front door. I feel the back of my head slam into the stairs—pain—and he's squeezing my neck with his left hand. I'm gasping for breath. He threatens me. He shows me a knife in his right hand and says not to fight him or scream. I feel like passing out. He's so angry, and he wants to hurt me. Why? I think he wants to kill me!*

The man puts his private part in my private area. It hurts. Now he's looking at his knife. I feel something, and I don't know why, but I think it's death. I can feel death. It's palpable even though I don't have a memory of feeling it before. I won't forget the look of darkness in his eyes as he reaches to cut my throat. He's driven to kill, and my terror is so unimaginable I have to leave my body in order to survive.

At this point something is happening that's hard to explain, but I believe it's God taking over. A light of love fills me, the rapist, and the room. For a moment, that is all I can see—light. It's a pure white light that doesn't strain my eyes. It's graceful. It's nothing I have any memory of ever seeing before. It's not of this Earth. I can't feel anything but love—a love so powerful it makes what I call love on Earth seem like nothing compared to it. Now, I can see the rapist through the light as he hesitates and looks confused. He just can't do it, and he abruptly gets up and leaves. Dear God, thank you! **(DEEP BREATH)**

[While remembering this attack, I thought my heart would stop.

The attacker wanted to seal the deal and make sure I wouldn't talk.]

After the flashback ended, I realized as an adult that my child self had come face to face with death. I believe I experienced Divine Intervention during this event, and it was my first experience with the power of Divine Love and how no darkness or evil can exist in God's loving presence. I'm so grateful my life was spared.

I also realized that during this rape I had dissociated again and experienced a dreamlike, robotic state. Once again, I had forgotten what happened, although I repeatedly dreamed of this rape over many years. I discounted the dream even though it was deeply disturbing and felt so real. My first therapist discounted it too. Once I consciously remembered this rape through the flashback, it explained why I would feel panicked and get really angry when someone would show up at my door unannounced. It was such an overreaction to a simple event and totally uncharacteristic of my normal behavior.

As I thought more about this flashback, I suspect the perpetrator of this rape was a man I didn't know who lived near the entrance to my neighborhood. My sense was of him stalking or hunting his prey. In hindsight, I believe his raping me had nothing to do with sex. Rape isn't sex; it's a violent crime! It had everything to do with taking his rage out on a vulnerable target.

Use of alcohol or drugs at an early age can be a sign of trauma such as sexual abuse.

—Darkness to Light[1]

1 "Child Sexual Abuse Statistics," Darkness to Light, accessed November, 28, 2017, http://www.d2l.org/the-issue/statistics.

As an adult looking back on my childhood, I connected this rape trauma to my smoking and drinking when I was nine or ten, and I believe this started after the second sexual trauma. Stores sold me cigarettes, and sometimes I told them they were for my parents. I took alcohol from my parents' liquor cabinet, and by the time I was twelve years old, I got older teens to buy it for me. I can't imagine my children drinking alcohol and smoking at nine or ten years old, but I understood that I had begun living with a survival mentality, which included a need to be numb in order to keep my rage and trauma memories hidden from myself. The self-numbing with alcohol and cigarettes caused me to slowly lose interest in normal activities and led me into a decline of inner darkness that I wanted no one to know about. I believed deep inside that I was bad; if anyone knew the truth about me, I would be unlovable. Why else would bad things keep happening to me?

Here is a picture of my adolescent self after the home assault. I can see the sadness in my eyes.

* * *

Since the flashbacks started, I intermittently experienced phases of memory flashes. In my early forties, I was home one day washing the dishes and feeling on edge. I started having memories from when I was twelve. I stood staring out the window at the beautiful sugar maple with its bright red and yellow fall leaves, lightheartedly waving in a gentle breeze. They began to fade from my view, and I found myself reminiscing about my adolescent life at my family's summer home in the Poconos. I slipped into the past.

I remembered that I spent a lot of time alone outdoors because my sisters had their own interests, and I didn't like sitting at home by myself. The neighborhood kids weren't around like they were at our main home, so a friend wasn't always available. I was an active child with now-obvious reasons to keep myself distracted by being busy. I liked to walk through the green patches of ferns, picking wild blackberries and blueberries on my way to one of my favorite places—the frog pond. I loved the sweet smell of the berries and their fresh taste. I'm right back there.

I'm wandering around on my family's motor scooter, and I head over to the horseback riding barn where I volunteer so I can ride horses for free. The barn is in a heavily wooded and secluded area at a lake community not far away. *OH NO!* I'm feeling a sense of dread and spaciness coming on. Another flashback?

> **(SHIELDS UP)** *I'm cleaning out a horse stall while the other worker is leaving on a trail ride. I see a dirty, ugly, gaunt man coming into the barn, and I feel on high alert! I'm thinking he must have been watching because as soon as the trail group leaves, he comes right in. I glance at his face and immediately know why he's here. He has a look I know!*
>
> [I was sadly familiar with that stalking, disturbed look the other rapists had, and I felt overcome with such horror and disbelief that I was dealing with rape again.]
>
> *I think to myself, What, do I have a sign on my head that says, "I'm a piece of shit, come threaten and rape me?" He's pushing me up against the wall now. I'm sliding back down. He's dragging me and pulling my pants down.*

> *I can sense my terror turn to rage as I swing at his face. My head is slammed into the floor, and it's no use—I stop fighting and lie there, taking in all my pain, humiliation, shame, and hatred of life. He's raping me, and I'm floating out of my body. His diseased-looking body is upon me, and now he is threatening to kill me if I don't keep my mouth shut. He's leaving now. I get up very slowly, like a robot, and go to my scooter to ride home. HOPELESSNESS. I'm hopeless. THERE'S NO WAY OUT OF THIS CYCLE!*
>
> [I don't remember ever going back there again.]

Okay, I've repressed a lot! I thought to myself at that point. Is it possible there's more hidden in my mind? How powerful must the mind be to hide all these rapes?

I awoke one morning in a devastated state after having another bad time with nightmares of being stalked and raped without finding anyone to help me, but I managed to get up and get my children ready for their school day. My body was moving slowly, grappling with feelings of deep despair. I kept thinking, *Just get them safely to school and then you can fall apart … hang in there … you must hold on and keep going.* I managed to get the kids to school, but while I was driving home, my state worsened.

THAT HORRIBLE FEELING OF DREAD AND SPACINESS! It was returning. But I couldn't stop it, and I found myself in another flashback from my main childhood home:

> **(SHIELDS UP)** *I'm around thirteen years old—in middle school. This is the year my father backs out of his marriage to my mother for good, leaving me feeling even more vulnerable.*
>
> *Just like a lot of other adolescent girls, I want attention from boys. I can go*

to my friend's house at the other end of the neighborhood and play flirtatious basketball with my friend and her brother's friends, who are in high school. How cool are my friend and I to be getting attention from high school boys? I feel older and special.

Today, my friend and her family are out for the day. I'm passing by her house, and I see some of the regular high school boys playing basketball. Something feels different today, but I'm not sure what it is. Should I leave? The boys are even rougher than usual. Why are they whispering to each other? A couple of them look mad and are leaving. Oh, the three that stayed are calling me to come around the back of the house. Okay, that's weird. But they're my friends, right? I'm going like the people-pleasing girl that I am.

*As I come around the corner, they grab me, pushing my head and the front of my body up against the sliding glass door. Oh no, I can see a reflection in the glass of my mashed face with my right eye bulging. It's so disturbing! No, not again! Please no, not this again. I'm being pulled around, and my face is held down on the patio table. They're laughing at me, telling me awful things like how I'm a pig and I want them to f*** me, and that I could just let them know when I want another f*** anytime.*

The three teen boys are raping me one at a time while the other two hold me down. They're jeering at me, calling me a slut and a whore and saying, "We know why you came here today, you want this—don't pretend you don't." LIES! I know what the truth is! I want to feel cool hanging out with older boys and getting attention. I DON'T want the awful pain of being shoved into a sliding glass door, thrown down against a table, painfully raped three times, verbally abused, humiliated, and shamed. What I do want is a cute high school boyfriend to go out on dates with, not to be treated like a nonexistent piece of worthless meat to be used and thrown away. I feel BROKEN!

I'm in total disbelief and confusion. Why did this happen? They're leaving. I feel my body sliding to the ground. Mechanically, I crawl to the side of the house. I sit, trying to collect myself. I'm dissociated. I can't feel anything, and I'm unsure if I can find my way home, which is only a short distance down a road I've traveled countless times. I'm walking home on autopilot like a deflated, soulless object.

[The rape memory disappeared before I started home, and my rage was so great it had to be hidden deep inside because it was too scary to live with.] **(DEEP BREATH)**

I realized as an adult that this rape was the event that sparked my fear of *myself*. I couldn't trust anything about myself, certainly not my judgment. This was all too much, and it jeopardized my ability to cope. How long could I hold all that pain inside? That assault was particularly rough for me because those rapists were my peers and I knew them, but to this day, my mind won't let me remember their names or faces. They feel familiar, and I do have memories of playing basketball with a group of high school boys. Still, I can only recall my friend's brother, who wasn't there the day I was raped.

* * *

I'd been having flashbacks for over a year by this time. They were spaced apart by months. I experienced the following remembering event with the associated traumatic feelings, whereas in the other visual memories, I would be numb while I observed the memory fragments some time after the initial flashback. Because of that, I was worried about losing it. It was so raw and fresh; it felt as if it were happening right in the present moment.

(SHIELDS UP) *I'm between ten and thirteen years old. I'm walking* *toward the woods to have a smoke, and a man gets my attention. I think his house backs up to the woods. He's luring me to his house with something about kittens and music he's giving away. This part is not clear. I don't think I recognize the man. Wait, it may be the neighborhood man who attacked me at my house on previous occasions, someone with a dark energy and behaviors that seem familiar to me. The repeat offender?*

It seems especially difficult to remember this attacker because it's a particularly brutal attack. I don't know how he gets me in his house. Am I even in his house? Is he disguised? Maybe I'm repressing his attacks so much that I can't recognize him. I want to know so damn bad, but I can't reach all of it. It's incredibly hard to believe I would trust anyone at this point, but I do. Between my broken judgment, gullibility, and love of animals and music, I unfortunately go with this person, and when I realize he is a bad man, it's just too damn late.

I'm in his house, excited to see something. Then suddenly, paralyzing fear hits me as I'm walking down his dark basement stairs. I'm so scared that I can't run. It's like I'm paralyzed or a robot in a state of terror walking in a dream. As soon as we get to the bottom of the cellar stairs, he puts a knife to my neck and pulls my hair in a bunch at the top of my head. He pushes me against the cold cellar wall. He says, "if you tell anyone, I'll come after you and slice you up When I'm done with you I'll slice up your mother, father, sisters, and dog too". He gives details. If I don't do what he wants me to do, he will kill me right now. It feels like he's going to rip my hair out.

He punches my lower abdomen, which makes my legs buckle. I fall to my knees. The picture of my young face shows unimaginable fear and pain—it's just awful and inconceivable. No wonder I put this memory so far away that I couldn't reach it for many years!

I'm watching as if my memory is a movie being shown to me, but I feel completely connected to the fact that it's me. I periodically cry out, cough, gag, and shake as I watch my memory of him orally raping me. I keep gagging, and my jaw is killing me. It's so, so disgusting! No wonder I need to vomit. It's the most repulsive sight! The attacker is pushing my upper body down to the floor, and then he continues to rape me. When I cry out in pain, he threatens me and covers my mouth or presses the knife into my neck. He, like the other rapists, is saying awful things to me about being a whore. He's telling me to crawl on my hands and knees to the stairs. He kicks me down, telling me to get going, and then he pushes me down again. More raping. I'm having trouble breathing, and I cry out. He pushes my face into the floor and growls loudly, "SHUT UP, BITCH!"

I can see the cellar door now, and I'm so afraid that if it closes, it's all over for me. He seems to be done, and I struggle to get up. I must be in shock, but he wants me to jump up and leave. I'm stumbling because my legs won't work right, and I keep falling. I feel disoriented. He pushes me out his back door and reminds me of what he will do to me and my family if I open my big slut mouth. I slowly make my way to the woods to collect myself. Then I walk home in a trance and fall asleep in my great escape—my bed. (**DEEP BREATH**)

* * *

Take a moment to do a *check-in* with yourself to see how you're doing. If you're feeling off-center or triggered, you can tune into yourself and focus on the present moment. See your surroundings, feel the seat you're in or the floor you're standing on, hear the sounds from this moment, and sense what your emotional state is. Are you feeling okay? You can reassure yourself with self-talk; remind yourself that what you just read is not your experience and you don't have to take it on as your own. You are safe, and you can ground yourself in this moment at your current age. Please take a couple of deep breaths.

Have you had flashbacks, and did you have them with the visual, physical, and emotional parts all at once? If you have, you understand the enormity of how devastating reliving an assault can be. It's just horrible!

Let's move on. From the last rape when I was around thirteen to my college years, I worked hard at school and became good at keeping my self-medicating behaviors under the radar. I was a good kid who had many secrets and bad habits.

The above flashbacks were spread out over a two-year period. In all, I had six, five of which I've detailed above. I did have another full-length flashback and mini-flashbacks, which I will talk about later, without the rape details.

All of the flashbacks happened decades after the attacks. *Prior to these, I had absolutely no memory of the events.* The rape flashbacks left me feeling taken down to nothing, broken, robbed, terrorized, shamed, and violated beyond belief. I didn't write about all the details of each rape; rather, I wanted to write about the rapists' behaviors and my responses to those behaviors. Some details of the rapes were necessary to share, in order to help you understand the depth of my trauma and the ensuing damage they caused. These details are associated with various experiences I had while going through the healing process, which I'll discuss later. It all fits together like a puzzle.

After experiencing the flashbacks, I was in a hypervigilant state, and my thoughts always returned to the question: What else happened to me?

Will these things ever stop? I wondered. *Is it possible for someone to recover from all of this damage?*

It's really hard to believe that I'll ever have any peace and healing.

Little Marie and Her Shadow

Inner Child and Shadow Healing Work

(20–37 years old)

PART I

Starting Therapy

Fortunately, I had psychological therapy prior to the onset of the flashbacks. In fact, I had been in therapy on and off for *fifteen years* before they occurred. The therapy I had begun when I was twenty-eight laid a lot of the foundation that made me strong enough to remember.

What prompted me to start therapy in the first place? Ironically, it was *not* because I wanted help dealing with issues. Rather, it was a simple curiosity related to a career change I was making. I also wanted help figuring out some dreams I was having—these were not traumatic, only extremely vivid. They always had something to do with water. My body would be gliding swiftly across a body of water, while sheets of rain came down on me, or I'd be swimming underwater and breathing through gills, or I'd have the recurring dream about the tidal wave. The swimming underwater dream was my favorite. I felt calm and free while under the water.

I graduated from college with a Bachelor of Science degree in computer science and went right to work in the computer software industry as a defense contractor. I was traveling and making good money. However, it was not fulfilling, and after getting married in my late twenties, I decided to change careers.

When I was twenty-five years old and living with my dad, my maternal grandmother, and my oldest sister, my dad died from advanced emphysema and double pneumonia. I adored my dad, and I was totally devastated at losing him. After he left my mom for good when I was thirteen years old, we had more opportunities to spend time together and got much closer. I still miss him and will always remember his loving fatherly eyes.

After my father's death, one of my mentors in the computer science field left to become a psychologist, and since I too was interested in psychology and helping others, I decided to work toward a master's degree in social work. For career purposes, I thought I needed to know what it was like to be a client in therapy, so my mentor put me in touch with one of her doctoral professors, a Jungian psychotherapist named Georgette. She was a tall fair-skinned woman with bright-blue eyes, beautiful white shoulder-length hair, and a soothing voice. During our first session, Georgette asked me to describe my childhood. Unbelievably, I said that it was great (and I meant it), but that I had no recollection of it prior to age twelve. Hmm, how did I know it was great if I couldn't remember? Not surprisingly, at that point she agreed to take me on as a client.

Our initial discussions were about the parts of my life that I could remember. I described how in my teens I was smoking, drinking, and taking drugs, and how my twenties mainly consisted of finishing college, working, and partying.

Without knowing the underlying reasons, Georgette realized that I was numbing myself, and she helped me to begin finding my sense of self by connecting to what I was feeling. During our work together, I focused on identifying a feeling I was having and then sitting with it without going blank. Each time any charged emotion was invoked, I went blank over and over again. Can you relate to that level of disconnection with yourself? I had been disconnected for so long it was all I knew. It was time to connect to myself, so I could connect more deeply with others; I hoped one day to be a good wife and mother. I would get frustrated with myself because I really wanted to know how I felt, but it was a skill I never used; I was probably stuck at a very early developmental stage in terms of connecting to my emotions. Little did I know that this "connecting with self" work would take years.

The skill I had the most practice with was *intellectualizing*—analyzing the hell out of everything. I have a naturally analytical mind and, boy, did I go to town with that one. Later, I learned that analyzing is a *defense mechanism* (i.e., if I'm so busy thinking about a problem, there isn't any room for feeling it and working through it). I used it to keep myself stuck by not feeling or moving through an authentic experience of life. But, truthfully, I needed to connect my thoughts to my feelings, my head to my heart. All you intellectualizers out there, I hope you're taking this message in.

During the time I was in therapy, I began keeping a journal, which I also found to be very therapeutic. Writing about my experiences became an effective way of learning how to experience my feelings and a vehicle for expressing them. Journaling is a wonderful tool for writing and drawing as part of one's healing process.

As I progressed in therapy, I knew I had to make my connection work come first. I was so focused on what was happening around me that I couldn't focus on me. I guess that would be too risky since I might start remembering I was raped before I was equipped to handle it. To that end, I started working on separating from my family of origin because we had a "fused" family system. The fusion dynamic is another way of describing a family without healthy boundaries between family members. I was overly focused on them and didn't seem to know how to care for myself and let them care for themselves, which is a trait of codependency.

I didn't know how to give healthy support to my family members without trying to control them, becoming overbearing, and giving of myself until I was ready to drop. I obsessed about how to solve their problems, which included running over to their homes to save the day at the drop of a hat. I had my own life with my loving husband, and I needed to focus my energies there. After getting married, I wanted to be present for my husband, but I found myself always responding to my family of origin. In doing so, I failed to understand where my responsibility ended and where theirs began. During this time, I had a lot of dreams about others just barging into my house and taking over. The crowd was running my life, and I felt insignificant and ungrounded. I didn't have healthy boundaries or my own private space. I observed how my husband maintained a healthy space with his relationships but noticed him keeping an exaggerated distance from my family. I believe now that he was compensating for my lack of healthy boundaries.

The following is a journal entry from when I was thirty-two. It describes part of the separation process I was undertaking with my family of origin.

> *I can only be part of their support, not all of it. Someone to listen, someone to reassure and love them. I can't fix them or their situation. The responsibility I put on myself to help them takes*

over my life. I can, however, make my own choices in life. I must keep my boundaries strong. I'm coming home to myself and setting myself free from the external world of family and society's rules and needs that I have allowed to control me. Their way is no longer my way. I'm finding my way one step at a time.

I cried when I read that entry fifteen years later. A feeling of elation welled up in me as I realized how far I'd come. It's just so hard to see progress when it's inching forward. Gratitude filled my heart. Though this was a major milestone, my healing journey was only beginning; I was only just becoming aware of what healthy thinking was and trying to develop it myself. It took some time and practice before I could implement healthy separation behaviors with my family.

I begin my healing journey here because I know that boundary and codependency issues are common among survivors of abuse. Are you aware of codependent behaviors in your life? If you have them, I hope you can let go of the behaviors that drive you *to override your needs in order to satisfy others*. You deserve to be first on your priority list because putting yourself first makes you stronger, helps you feel better, and makes you more effective to those around you.

I continued to move from black-and-white thinking of codependency and being out of touch with myself to finding *my* voice and integrating the compartmentalized parts of me that had been locked away in separate memory boxes in my mind. I kept reminding myself that there isn't always a right or wrong answer and that I needed to continue checking in with myself, in order to develop a stronger sense of self. I would practice by writing down what I was working on onto Post-it Notes and sticking them on things around my house as reminders to ask myself …

What is best for my family and me? What do I want? If it works for me, feels comfortable, and feels right, then that is what I'm allowed to choose. If it doesn't fit what others think, then too bad; they can struggle with it. It's not mine, and I have to let the binding, smothering crap of others' opinions go! Why am I trying to fit someone else's mold when I want to build my own?"

PART II

Meeting My Inner Child

I kept forging ahead, making progress in finding myself and continuing the separation work with my family of origin. My husband was supportive; he just seemed to have an intuitive sense of where healthy lines should be when it came to my family.

Quite unexpectedly, at thirty-two years old and during my first pregnancy, I started a new phase concerning my inner child. For the first time, I became aware of my younger self one day while meditating on a recliner in my living room. As I closed my eyes, I saw her but didn't yet realize who she was. *Who is that?* I thought. Afterward, I journaled the following:

> *I see a child in my mind. Who is she, why is she with me, and why does she look dead? I feel uneasy and agitated. I'm opening my eyes and trying to calm down. I'm getting worried. Am I going nuts?*

I discussed this experience with my therapist, who recognized it and explained it as Inner Child Work (ICW). She said, "Marie, you're embarking on ICW." What a relief! I wasn't hallucinating and going insane. Each time I saw her, my child self would either have tears streaming down her face, be red with rage, or have a lifeless look in her eyes. I would speak to her in my mind and ask what was wrong. One day, seemingly agitated, she actually answered me, saying she was afraid because there wasn't enough love for her with the baby on the way.

In therapy, I worked on having my adult self explain to my younger self, who I began calling Little Marie, that she was valuable, and that my adult self would take care of her, as well as the baby that was on the way. After that, when I noticed I was feeling distressed on occasion, I would work on visualizing my adult self holding my child self and asking what she needed. Sometimes throughout the day, I would picture myself carrying her around in a sling to comfort her. My therapist suggested holding my child self when I was flooded with emotion, so I could see her in my lap and not let her take over. This helped me to react in a more adult fashion.

Visualizing communicating with my younger self was a helpful tool for me. Many times, when people are experiencing an intense emotion, it's a sign that the child self is on the surface. People usually don't act their adult age when their upset child self is calling the shots. Recognizing this, and lovingly working with that part of the self, can create a powerful shift in a positive direction and help us gain our composure. Acknowledging our child self and helping him or her feel taken care of goes a long way in healing our unmet childhood needs. These needs do not disappear when we become adults. They usually show up in unhealthy ways of behaving, such as addictions and codependency, which wreak havoc throughout our lives.

Connecting with my inner child seemed to start on its own, but I'm guessing my therapy had brought me to a point where I was ready to embark on the next leg of my healing journey. Little did I know that inner child work would be a pivotal part of my healing. Its timing also had something to do with the pregnancy; the fact that I was pregnant represented my baby but also symbolized the birthing of my healing. It was bringing my past closer to the surface, and it was painful but miraculous, just like the physical birthing of my son.

From then on, I would occasionally become aware of my younger self during quiet times. Till this day, I still sense her, just not as frequently. Over time, I realized that certain situations and strong emotions bring her to the surface. That's her telling me she needs comfort and safety.

Note: During childhood, our child self is formed and lives within our minds for the rest of our lives. There are parts of healing that are unique to working with our inner child and are very important for those of us who were traumatized at a young age. Part of working with our inner child is to recognize how we may have gotten split off into different age compartments or in different identities.

Parts of our development were most likely interrupted, or even stopped at the ages at which trauma occurred, and these parts are forever split off, painful parts of our childhood selves. This childlike part of oneself needs help healing its wounds and being re-parented by the adult self. Do you ever have an awareness of your younger self? If so, do you notice his or her presence at certain times?

My ICW also included a tool I call a "re-do." This involved visualizing a replay of baby moments with my mother, but you can work on a re-do for any points in your life. For example, I would imagine my mother holding, cherishing, and breastfeeding me—sometimes even sleeping with me. When she picked me up, I felt the chaos leave, and I calmed down. It was everything I wanted. It was something my baby self yearned for, and it made me feel good to do this work. As time went on, when I comforted my child self, she would have joy in her eyes, and she looked so moved that I cared for her. Simultaneously, this gave my adult self hope. I was embarking on a journey of re-parenting my child self and learning how to love *me*.

At times, though, I was unwilling to be comforting with myself and would feel resistant and angry. I found my resistance to be quite frustrating and learned over time that *the more I accepted my mental states, the quicker I moved through them.* Instead of denying and numbing my feelings, I could let them wash through me like a wave while I gave them permission to be with me. In my acceptance, I could let them go, but in my denial and stuffing them down, I was allowing them to hold me prisoner.

* * *

In the beginning of doing ICW, I thought I was supposed to separate from my child self and leave her in the past (i.e., that she needed to die for good). Later I realized I was wrong about that and needed to comfort and mother her instead. The more the needs of my child self were met, the quieter this part of me became. This was a revelation!

The following journal poem describes the initial thought of leaving my child self behind:

LIVING IN THE VALLEY OF DEATH

I lay me down to sleep
To lie in the valley of death
In the pastures of days gone by

To let go of my wounded child self
And embrace my present self.

I hesitantly let go of the familiar feelings
Of torment, pain, and deprivation

As I let my child self go to die her death in present day
But to linger on eternally in the dark past of the time before
Deep within.

Goodbye, my love—you've been all I've known,
But now I'm grown and I'm safe, loved, and becoming whole,
My love, goodbye.

****

Here is a picture that goes with the above poem, called *Dead Self.* It's my adult self carrying my dead younger self:

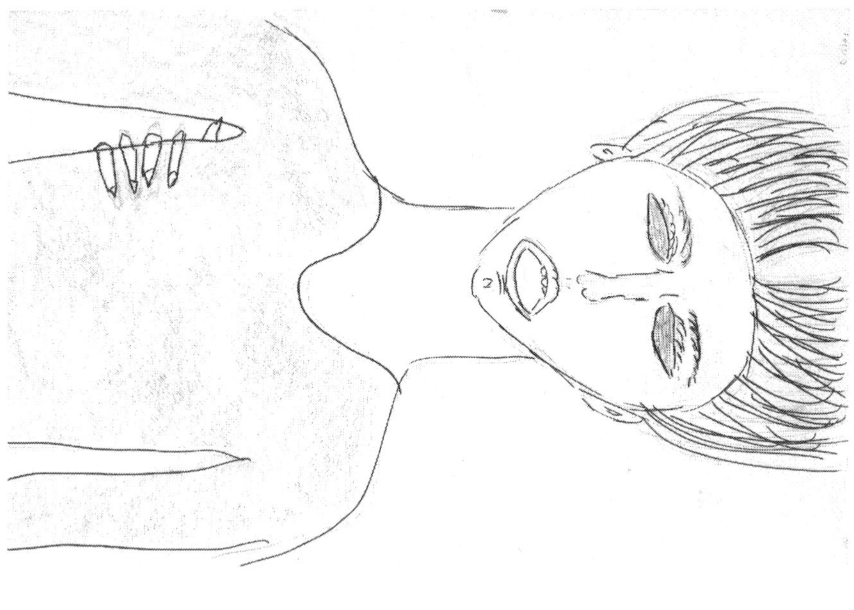

****

I'm so thankful I was discovering a wise inner self and had a caring therapist guiding me through this crucial stage of healing.

During the time of beginning my ICW, my son was born. His birthing was traumatic for both of us, which activated an unknown posttraumatic stress disorder (PTSD) in me. Unfortunately, no one recognized it. I believe the reason why my son's delivery was traumatic, and not merely difficult, was because it triggered old hidden trauma. And that hidden raw energy was what I was unknowingly dealing with. I think the PTSD was triggered due to a combination of the extreme pain I was in during labor, the hours-long pushing stage, and a male doctor lying across my stomach to apply what is called *fundal pressure.* The fundal pressure popped my son out and damaged my body. I was screaming and punching the doctor because I unconsciously experienced his abrupt tactics as an attack. Why no one explained to me beforehand what was going to happen, I just don't understand. Anyway, when the doctor was lying over my abdomen to force my baby out in an attempt to avoid an emergency C-section, it triggered my trauma. I hit his back and cursed him while somewhere in my mind I was punching my rapists. However, I will say that even though I experienced a lot of physical and emotional distress during the birth, I also experienced so much joy getting to see my son and hold him for the first time. He was bright, joyful, and oh so cute! What a beautiful gift.

Once my PTSD was activated, though, my joy was tempered, and I was in rough shape for a long time. (See Appendix D, Trauma Education and Triggers, for a description of PTSD symptoms.) I began having awful episodes where I would curl up in the fetal position. It would feel like I was floating and consumed with despair. I would ask myself, "Where am I, and what is happening?"

These experiences would leave me feeling numb and disconnected. There were no pictures in my mind, just sensations (body memories) and emotional memories. The body stores trauma memories at a cellular level, and a certain touch or sound, and even healing work can trigger an involuntary physical response, such as curling up into a fetal position, avoidance behaviors, pain, or lashing out. Working with my therapist, I realized that I was having in-utero flashback memories. Only years later did I come to understand these memories were of me as a fetus experiencing my mother's depression and her desire to die. She had told me she wanted to die when she was pregnant with me, an event that was unplanned, because she and my father were in the midst of serious marital troubles. During a troubled time in her life, my pregnant mother fantasized about drowning herself. *Click!* The pieces began fitting together to expose what those in-utero flashbacks were about. I grieved for us both and felt bad about our suffering together. Having these memories answered a longstanding question I had about whether unborn children are aware and able to remember.

Once my PTSD was triggered, I also had memories of being a baby on a bed flailing my limbs in distress. There was no mommy "container," and I felt so alone and chaotic that I felt like I was specks of energy all over the room. My memories were of my beloved mother always near or walking by but never coming to me. It seemed like she didn't acknowledge my presence, and I felt like I was an object or a doll. In those memories, I desperately needed my mother; I felt unworthy that the mother I loved refused to pick me up and stare into my eyes with adoring love. My mother had no idea this was happening. Knowing what I know now, I believe if Mom had known, she would have tried to connect with me more.

As a new mom, I struggled to be a mother to my own infant son while coping with PTSD, and the seemingly bottomless pit of my unfulfilled childhood needs. And crazy exhausted from it all! My nervous system was completely on edge, and my immune system was pretty much nonexistent, so I got sick a lot. I would easily feel overwhelmed then explode with anger, which would morph into guilt and shame. I was so consumed by what was going on internally that others' needs felt like an attack, which in turn triggered my trauma. What a mess.

Some of the anger episodes, or temper tantrums, were so intense that they made me feel out of control. I have a vivid memory of feeling full of rage for what seemed like no reason. I was in my bathroom one day while I was home alone with my toddler. I wanted to rip the walls apart with an axe as seething rage took over my being. I was trying to get my son out of the bathroom, knowing my intense energy was scaring him. I was yelling and crying and moving him out the door so I could close it, but he repeatedly and frantically grabbed back onto my leg with his whole body. His poor little face was confused and terrified. It was just awful for us both. His distress finally snapped me out of my state, and I surrendered to his need to be with me. We sat on the floor sobbing as I held him. I told him I was sorry and that he hadn't done anything wrong.

I'm grateful my uncontrolled anger was not directed at my child. Explosive rage is a symptom of PTSD, and it seemed to come out of nowhere. All of the hypervigilant and overreactive behaviors I was experiencing were directly related to my frazzled nervous system, the PTSD, and the rapes. The anger pushed down my sadness, and the sadness was a blanket that lay over my fear. The following is a journal entry about my sadness and anger at that time:

> *Sadness is such a deep pain that goes into the bowels of my being. It hurts so much! It's dark, scary, very painful—it's no wonder I push it away with anger. No! You can't come up; my big wall of rage will stop you.*

I found out over time that I had to face my darkness and go into it in order to find my light. I wrote the following poem about doing this:

Who Am I

I have to go into my pain to find my peace
Go and seek my void
My darkness
My fear
There I will find my light
My peace
My love
My spiritual self

****

At this point in my adulthood, my child self regularly expressed her fear of being alone. That fear would lead to self-medicating with food. My old unsatisfied needs and fears provided the urge to eat compulsively. I just didn't know what else to do since I was used to engaging my childhood coping skills.

Wanting to try something other than food, I tried meditating and asking God to help me see my greatest fear. I went into a deep meditative state and could sense myself falling into a black void, for what seemed like a long time, and felt panicked. When I came out of my meditation, I wrote this poem about the void experience:

The Void

Welcome to the void
Where pain reigns and fear is always
Nothing but darkness
Abandonment
Aloneness
Emotional deprivation
Cold
Terror
Shaking
Quaking with fear
Screaming for help
Oh God, help me
Someone help me
I'm lost, discarded
Nothing, nothing, nothing
I'm falling, no one here
Not even self
Just nothing

****

Can you identify with the poem's essence of emptiness and aloneness? Writing the poem helped me realize some of my deeper core feelings and beliefs. After writing the poem, I drew this face, which had come out numerous times over several years. I would sit down to draw with my son or on my own, and the face pictured on the following page would appear repeatedly. I eventually realized it was the emotional anguish within me.

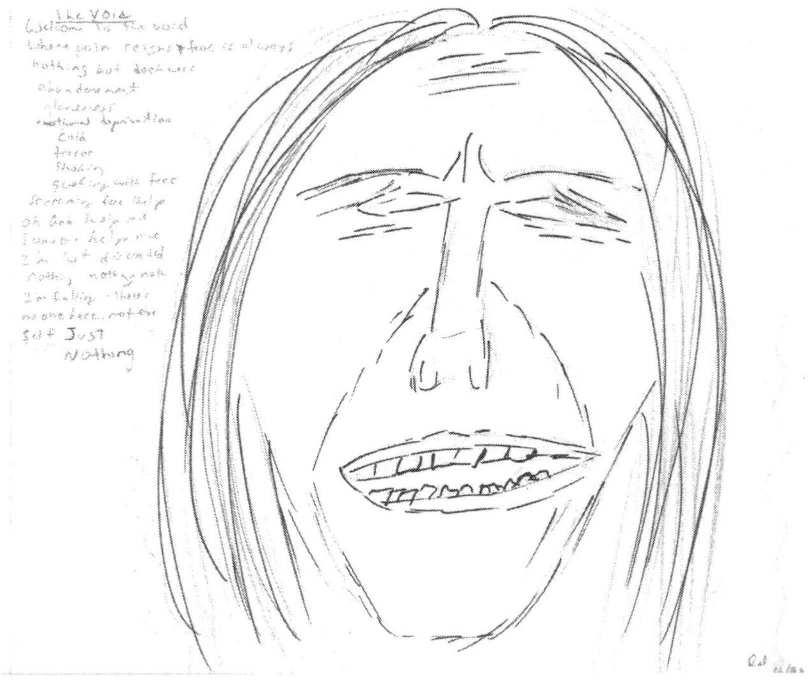

****

As I was falling through the void during my meditation, I eventually, and ever so gently, landed in a huge right hand and peacefully surrendered. Ahhh … I felt safe and loved, and I knew it was God's hand. I understood that my greatest fear was being abandoned or forsaken. I wasn't alone, and God was always with me, waiting for me to know that truth.

A few years later, I read a Bible passage talking about how God's right hand will deliver you, and I was floored because it reminded me of my meditation. "Though I walk in the midst of trouble, you preserve me … you stretch out your hand, and your right hand delivers me" (Psalm 138:7, NRSV). After the poem, I drew this picture:

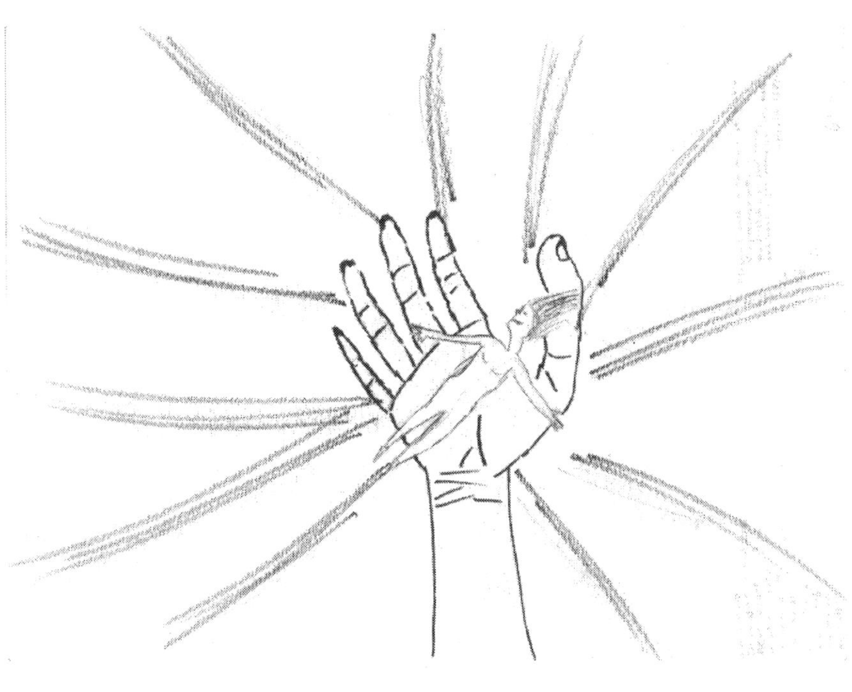

****

Twelve years later, the void vision inspired me to write this prayer/poem:

The Long Road Home

Each time I endure what appears unendurable
God is waiting for me with His Love
Not more pain
Not punishment
But Love
When I fall into the void of what I think is unimaginable terror
What do I find?
Nothing
Not even self
Then I finally land—His right hand delivers me
And gently I lay in peace and know Love once again
All healing roads eventually lead to Him
God was always there waiting for me
To know Him
To know Love

This poem is special because it reminds me that no matter what I think is happening, God is with me, waiting for me to let go of my fear and focus on Him instead, to focus on His strength and His peace instead of my fear. Most importantly, I was internalizing the truth that I'm never alone when I remember that spiritual support is always here when I choose to open up to it.

Note: I mention meditation a few times in my book, and I believe it's a powerful tool for learning to focus and quiet the mind and nervous system. It's a skill, which means it takes practice. Meditation has given me many beautiful healing experiences, and I highly recommend it as a healing tool. Just focusing on breathing for a few minutes is a great start. When you get distracted, try not to be frustrated with yourself; accept it and go back to your breath. Breathing deeply into your abdomen is calming. Meditation is worth every minute you put into it.

PART III

Discovering My Shadow Self

I had heard people speak of the shadow self for years but didn't have any concept of what that meant in my own life, but I was about to find out.

As my therapy continued, I grew more interested in delving into my mind. At thirty-six, I attended an Association for Spirituality and Psychotherapy (ASP) conference in Manhattan, where I picked up a Jung-inspired book called *Romancing the Shadow* by therapists Connie Zweig and Steven Wolf. Here are selected quotes describing the shadow self:

> Beneath the social mask we wear every day, we have a hidden shadow side: an impulsive, wounded, sad, or isolated part that we generally try to ignore, but which can erupt in harmful ways.[2]
>
> Within each woman and man, the dim cavern of the unconscious holds our forbidden feelings, secret wishes, and creative urges. Over time, these "dark" forces take on a life of their own, forming an intuitively recognizable figure—the shadow."[3] [Or shadow characters, as I describe below.]

---

2 Connie Zweig and Steve Wolf, *Romancing the Shadow* (New York: Ballantine Books, 1997), inside flap.

3 Zweig and Wolf, *Romancing the Shadow,* inside flap.

Another way of describing the shadow self is that it's where the dark and rejected parts of us get relegated to in our unconscious minds. These parts of ourselves were rejected by loved ones, or we felt too unsafe to show certain parts when we were young; since we wanted approval, they got shoved deep inside. My hidden rage was shoved into my shadow self, and since I was a master people-pleaser, there could be no rage on the surface. It had to be hidden.

As I began to explore my shadow by doing exercises from the book and contemplating the material, I wrote this in my journal:

Embracing My Shadow

In the shadow I hide
I am disowned—unloved—excommunicated
So dark where I roam
Must keep me hidden from the world
I shed tears in my loneliness
I rage at my unseen-ness
I grow bigger each passing forgotten day

I am shadow
Please call to me
Make me your own and love me
I am a powerful creative force

I am more gold than anything
See me and integrate me
We will soar together
Light and dark

****

Reading *Romancing the Shadow* helped me to accept what came up without being scared off. I practiced an exercise mentioned in the book about visualizing my higher self, or core self, at the head of a long table with my various shadow characters seated on each side.[4] The characters I saw seated around me were a female mother/protector/warrior, a male figure who drove people nuts with his tenacity, and another male figure who would steamroll right over anyone in a stressed-out and cut-off state. These were parts of myself that served survival purposes that I did not want to own.

At different times while working with the table exercise, my child self was sitting there slumped over and looking dejected. The hopelessness she exuded profoundly affected me. When I looked into her eyes, there was nothing—a soulless stare. What on earth could have caused that much devastation? It would be years till I would finally know my child self's truth.

This new awareness from using the table exercise helped me get a better understanding of my behavior. When I noticed myself acting out or feeling immature, I had a new tool. I would check out my shadow table in my mind's eye, and lo and behold, a shadow character or my inner child would be at the head of the table. Next, I would visualize my higher self sitting at the head. But first, I acknowledged the shadow character and told them how I knew they had helped me cope in the past and that I was grateful for their help. Of course, I knew they were just symbols of hidden parts of myself and talking to them in my mind was also symbolic. After using the shadow table tool, I usually felt noticeably calmer. This tool was an extension of connecting with myself.

4 Zweig and Wolf, *Romancing the Shadow*, 32.

The most powerful shadow character had two traits I really needed: a protective mother and a fearless warrior! How appropriate for my wounded baby and child selves to have this symbol as their protector shadow character. She symbolized the mother figure I needed, and she was also the scary you-don't-want-to-mess-with-me part that was rarely on the surface. I didn't want this part on the surface because it was downright scary.

While meditating one day, I saw something odd.

> *It's a secret, dark cave. There's a baby all alone in it, and it's lying on a dirt floor looking almost lifeless. Oh my gosh! Something tells me that baby is me. At the cave's entrance, there's a scary-looking woman. Who is she? It's the mother/warrior, and she's standing guard. I don't know why, but I am compelled to call this place the "womb cave." The woman feels powerful, but also threatening!*

As part of doing ICW in my mind, I chose to regularly take a few moments out of my day to care for my baby self by visiting her in the womb cave. I put down a thick fluffy pad for her to lie on, wrapped her in a blanket while holding her, and spoke to her as a loving mother while gazing into her lifeless eyes. Over time (years), my baby self was transformed from an almost-lifeless lump to a more awake, active, and normal infant. The process of experiencing this growth was very gratifying, and I knew I was making progress.

I also became a parent to my other younger parts and mothered them all. This new relationship between my adult self and younger parts created fertile ground for beautiful healing through loving acceptance, support, and protection.

As with any of the tools I've used, it takes time and practice to remember to use them, which led to using them more effectively. I used my Post-its approach to remind myself of what I was working on, like visiting the womb cave. There were some on the bathroom mirror, my bedroom dresser, the refrigerator, and kitchen table—yes, all over the place! Some days I would see a Post-it reminder and think, *I'm not doing that. I don't feel like it.* After many times of resisting and then being able to accept my resistance and give myself a break, I realized: *The more I accepted my resistance to tools and didn't beat myself up for it, the sooner the resistance would wane and an opening to helping myself would appear.*

Is it hard for you to get yourself to use healing tools and deal with your resistance? I think if we can see that whatever we're experiencing is there for a reason, then we can work toward accepting our feelings with patience and understanding. That's not easy to do, but it gets easier with practice.

PART IV

Compulsive Coping Behaviors, More Rage, and Pain

FOOD—FOOD—FOOD. I've had another night of dreams with rows of long banquet tables filled with every dish imaginable. I browsed every type of comfort food—mushy lasagna, chocolate cakes, and coffee ice cream with whipped cream, hot fudge, and Heath bar sprinkled over it. I ate everything I could get my hands on, filling a seemingly endless well, but not feeling full. When I woke up from these nights, I felt disgusted with myself, thinking —*Who does that? What the hell is wrong with me? I'm disgusting!*

At thirty-four years old, I couldn't stop thinking about food during my waking hours and even in my sleep—what I could eat, when I could eat, how much I could eat. Oh my God, I couldn't stop eating! I would look for times when I could be alone with my food. I thought it was my friend and my soother. I even dreamed about situations where I could be alone with food so no one could see my shameful behavior.

Binges consisted of times when I ate one thing after another in a fast and disassociated state. I would eat and eat and eat, and still I didn't feel full. Then suddenly, I would feel sick to my stomach and have to lie down. It totally shut me down and kept all my emotions at bay, except the one about hating myself for gluttonous behavior.

My binges seemed like missing blocks of time where I couldn't tell you what I was thinking or even what I ate.

In hindsight, I believe it was getting harder for me to repress my trauma memories as I got older and had more mommy responsibilities, so I ate to hold my memories and emotions down. I also understand now that compulsive or addictive behaviors are common among people who are avoiding trauma-related pain or PTSD. Without realizing it, my food obsession caused me to both run from and ruin my life. How could I escape this self-destructive prison?

I recognized that I needed help, and Overeaters Anonymous (OA) seemed to be the only place that would aid me in my struggle with food. They enabled me to give up self-medicating with food for a while. As a result, I began connecting more with the shadow, spiritual, creative, and feeling parts of myself.

During this time, I was getting really agitated, so I would take a moment and tune into myself either by meditating or just stopping what I was doing and checking in. I sensed Little Marie and connected with her in my mind. One day while tuning into myself, I saw Little Marie screaming at me: "How dare you take the only thing that I can control and soothe myself with?" She was furious! It felt like a violation to her because she believed food was her only tool to cope with her inner distress. My adult self taking that comfort from her felt like abandonment and punishment. *Aha! That's why I go to the food. My child self is on the surface trying to soothe herself and keep those feelings down.* This was an important moment of self-awareness in my journey.

Although I resolved to deal with my self-medicating, my struggle with food showed up on and off for many more years. The following quote is about compulsive eating, but it applies to any compulsion. It helped me see that overeating serves the purpose of not confronting emotions and that avoidance prevents one from facing their darkness and being able to heal.

> *You did not become an overeater for no reason. If you choose to honestly confront the emotions involved in both causing and healing your compulsive patterns, you will experience a dark night of the soul. But a dark night of the soul is ultimately a good thing, for it both precedes and prepares your spirit for rebirth.* ***The darkness is simply the revisiting of old feelings, in the absence of which true healing cannot occur.*** *It's important to remember that this darkness is temporary, and leads ultimately to the light beyond it.*
>
> —Marianne Williamson[5]

I love that quote! Over time and with more work, I noticed my eating urges and food dreams weren't around so much. The more I focused on comforting my inner child and reassuring her that my adult self would handle everything for her and protect her, the less activated she became and the less she wanted to overeat. She was learning that it was comfort and love she needed, not food.

Once my compulsive eating was held at bay for a good stretch of time, I started to really grow and connect with other parts of myself, like my creativity. I was home alone one day and feeling an inner push to journal, so I sat down at the kitchen table and wrote the following two poems, along with their drawings. I wonder if you can

5 Marianne Williamson, *A Course in Weight Loss: 21 Spiritual Lessons for Surrendering Your Weight Forever* (Carlsbad: Hay House Inc., 2010), 173.

relate to the lost feeling I express here, and I hope you can relate to the hopeful feelings too.

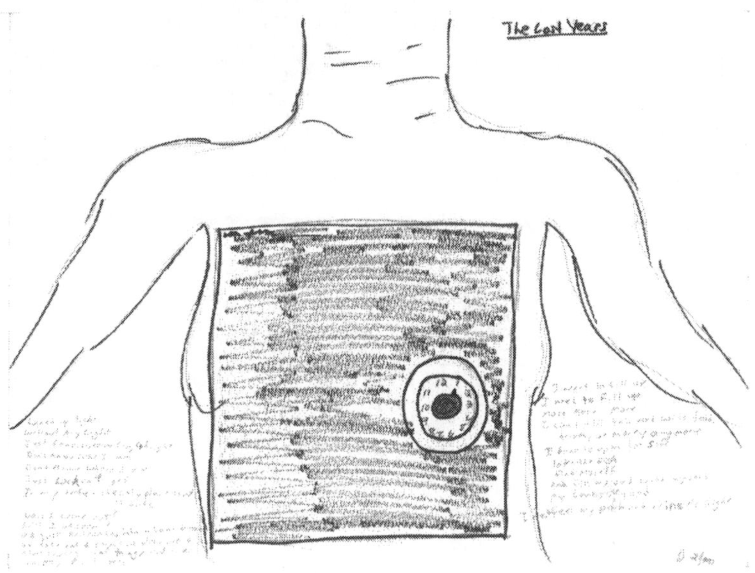

The Lost Years

Locked up tight
Without any light
Just fear disconnection and fright
Don't know who I am
Don't know where I am
Just locked up tight
In my safe the only place that is safe

Dare I come out?
Will I be seen?
Or just railroaded into a fake dream
Of external destructive pleasure
And other superficial things

****

This drawing and poem came right after *The Lost Years*.

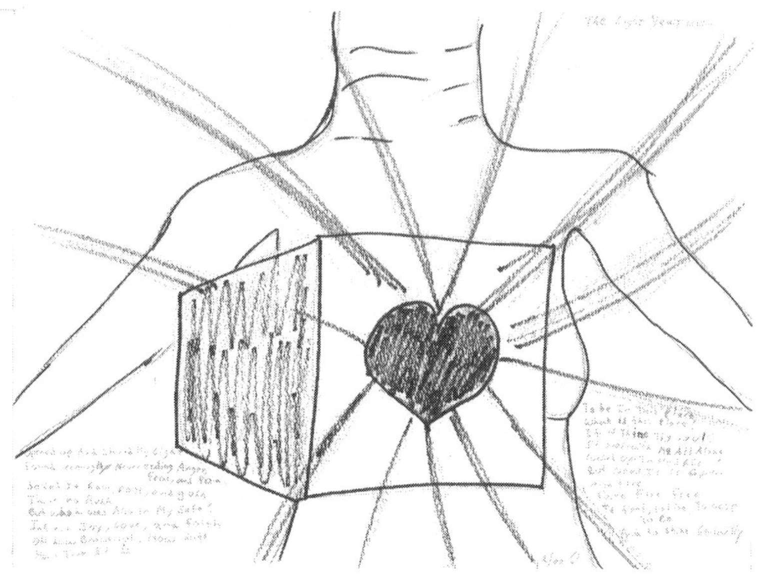

The Light Years

Opened up and shined my light
Found seemingly never-ending anger, fear, and pain
So let it rain, pour, and gush
I'm in no rush

But what else was in my safe?
Infinite joy, love, and faith
Oh how beautiful, how safe, how true it is
To be in this place

What is this place?
It is thine, thy spirit
It was with me all along
Locked up in my safe
But now it's open and free
Free

To feel, to live, to love
To be
And to shine eternally

****

The above poems were mirroring how my thoughts and behaviors were changing. I was feeling a connection to myself and to God. Each time I went within myself to check in with my younger parts or see if my adult self needed something, that reduced my eating urges and created an opening for other parts of me to be developed—like sensing God's presence or allowing creative energy to bubble up. I was amazed at how my loving connection with myself was inviting areas of strength into my daily life. When I would be in emotional pain, I could meet it with connecting to God or creatively expressing myself rather than acting out of self-hatred, like gorging my body with food.

This new relationship with God provided the strength I needed to keep going into the dark and painful places within me. The process of self-connection had led to a connection with my spiritual self. Oh, thank goodness, some progress!

My child self loved playing with my son. We would bring out the paint easel on the front porch and paint and paint and paint. It was so much fun! Sometimes we would run around the back deck blowing and chasing bubbles to see who could pop the most. Oh, and one of our favorites was when we went deep into imaginative play as we became pirates on the play set lookout tower. Even though I had many rough moments, we also had many more loving, affectionate, and playful times together. I'm so grateful.

The time spent in play with my son helped me to express myself creatively. Watching him engage in joyful painting filled my heart. All that time spent painting, drawing, and doing crafts pushed me to let go and create on my own, and it was a wonderful sense of release and self-connection tool! I had been shut down for so many years that experiencing myself as a flower slowly opening was deeply moving. I could draw anything I wanted, and it didn't matter if anyone thought it was good; I just loved drawing it. Drawing helped me release my pain. I was intrigued by whatever image came out, and it usually reflected something I felt deep within myself. It was so freeing to watch my heart emerging from my locked vault. How relieved I was to let the lost years go, but I still had that rage to cope with.

In the years leading up to remembering, my rage showed up as agitation or more extreme emotional states, like my bathroom memory with my son. One day I would feel anxious but okay, and the next I would feel angry. It seemed to come out of nowhere and made me feel on edge; everything I perceived went through a very negative filter. Everyone and everything just pissed me off, and this experience scared me. These periods ranged from days to weeks of inner torment. Even more, I hated how angry I felt around my loved ones, and I yearned for a break. Poems like the one below gave me hints about my anger, but I was still blocking myself from knowing why this rage was within me. I would usually get some relief after drinking enough alcohol to lower the death grip I had on my emotions, then I could just cry and release. My sobbing was the vehicle that released the pressure valve of anger that guarded my broken heart.

The most challenging part, aside from the resulting pain of my trauma, was the fear of my own rage. It was daunting! I needed to keep reassuring myself that my adult self was safe and could take care of my younger selves. Oh, and that saying, "There is nothing to fear but fear itself," is exactly right. My fear of my rage was far scarier than the rage itself! Please, don't let your fear of what you might find hold you back. You can make it through what's inside you. Do you have moments of rage or an ongoing agitation that plagues you from your childhood traumas?

When I was thirty-seven years old (six years before remembering my rapes), I wrote the following poem and drew a picture of my rage. I was perplexed by it. *Why is this with me?* Rage is a cruel reality for survivors of childhood sexual abuse. If you experience rage from your traumatic past, I pray for you to love yourself anyway and to be patient with yourself while you navigate through it, hopefully with professional help.

Rage

Rage is pain
The blanket that hides my suffering
The cover that destroys hurts and tears down
In my cry for help
My rage is my pain
Screaming out
See me—Feel my soul wounds
Before I explode or get lost in the void that numbs me

****

As time went on without food or alcohol to self-medicate with, devastating pain continued to bubble and ooze up inside me like a smoldering volcano. The pain manifested in the form of nightmares where I was vulnerable and ignored, like one where I found myself in a train station. I wasn't sure what I was doing there or where I was going, and I felt lost. On top of that, I realized I was totally naked, and I began crying. I tried calling out for help, but it was in vain, and no one came to my aid. I knew a man was stalking me. In the midst of a rush of people, I was totally ignored. Many other dreams had a man preying on my vulnerability. I would wake up from the nightmares feeling devastated and wanting to hide from this harsh, cold world under the covers of my bed.

Throughout this struggle, though, I kept holding onto God, asking Him for help, and seeing myself in His hand. Being able to depend on a power greater than myself felt hugely supportive; it was another form of self-love.

PART V

Learning How to Love Myself

Note: Instead of using the terms child self and *adult self*, going forward I will use CS and AS, respectively. Later, I'll use ADS for my adolescent or younger teen self.

The following are entries from a journal I kept while continuing with ICW. This work was such an important healing tool for my progress of integrating and forming internal allies with my split-off parts of self.

One day I became aware of how bully mode (a pushy state or the steamroller shadow character) showed up when anxiety, chaos, and stress would take hold of me. I asked myself: How can I be mindful of this dynamic, and what can I do? I told myself that at some point I do become aware of being in bully mode, and I can say STOP and ask: What do I need? Don't bully and instead talk nicely to myself. Not that angry, critical self-talk, but a tender, loving voice. I know when I do that for myself, then I can do that with others too. A kind inner voice strengthens, and a critical one weakens.

As I was observing my self-talk, I sensed my CS. My AS asked, "How are you, Little Marie?" CS replied, "I'm okay. I like it here in my new space, my real home (my real home being an experience of being seen and parented by God and my AS). I get scared a lot, and I want to hide, but you help me. You don't try to shut me up, and

> *you don't let me shut myself up with food and alcohol. Thank you, thank you for caring and for staying with me, for helping me. I love you. I'm hurt, you know. But with help, I'm learning where I can go for help, and that is you, AS, and God. You aren't leaving me. I really am safe. It's just hard to remember sometimes."*
>
> *My AS replied, "I can help you. I will try to remember to check in with you and be aware of bully mode because that is an indicator that you are upset and need comforting. I want to be there for both of us, big and little."*

Tuning into myself when I detected the presence of being pushy and responding with a listening, accepting presence really helped me stop and soften my behavior. That's amazing! The bully energy was my child self trying to get my attention, so my AS could ease her fears, and love and protect her. Just beautiful! I'm so grateful for this realization. Prior to this, I thought I was supposed to squash my inner critic, but that's the opposite of what quiets that part of me. A loving presence or response is what strengthens and shifts fear into feeling calm and safe.

As time went on, I saw how much connecting with my CS, parenting her, and giving her space for self-expression was helping quiet some of my inner chaos and angst. In fact, my ICW is a huge reason I'm doing so well. I've included many journal entries documenting this work to give you specific examples of what I mean by helping to heal the child within. Working with my CS from the past set the stage for healing in the present, like the following quote suggests:

Make peace with your past so it won't disturb your present
—Kate Swaffer[6]

Here's another ICW journal entry I wrote after waking and checking in with Little Marie one day:

"How are you, Little Marie?" She looked sad and came over to me and told me her hopes for Mom mothering her. My CS asked if Mom would do that today. My AS was taken aback by my CS's innocence and total lack of time awareness. She didn't know childhood was over. She was so hopeful, so ready to believe that Mommy will love her the way she needs to be loved today. CS asked, "Will she come today? Am I worth it enough now that she'll come today?" Wow, I realized why I would get so irritable when my mother visited. My CS would get seduced by her dream of a mother satisfying her needs, but instead would get ignored, feel so alone, and become wounded again. It was a destructive cycle that had been repeated for thirty-seven years.

My AS told my CS, "No, Little Marie. I'm so sorry, honey, but Mother isn't going to do that for you today. She never will. That time has passed, but I can mother you, cherish you, and protect you. It isn't that Mom doesn't want to, it's because you're an adult now, so she can't. I believe if she could give you what you so deeply want and need, she would. I want to help you accept that your dream with Mom will not happen, but God and I can help soothe you. I want to help you let go and finally have some peace my dear, sweet, beautiful child. It's time for us to move on and help each other. Can I mother you, Little Marie?" CS replied, "Yes, yes!"

Then my AS continued, "Let's learn together. I'll learn to check in

6 Kate Swaffer, "7 Cardinal Rules for Life," October 2, 2013, www.kateswaffer.com/2013/10/02/7-cardinal-rules-for-life/.

with you, and you can give me signals. You will get your needs met, and I will be able to move on and be present in my adulthood. If Mommy did what you wanted, what would she do?"

My CS got very excited and said, "She would sit right here next to me." (So my AS did that in my mind). "She would hug me, kiss me, and tell me she loves me, how she cherishes me, how I'm a beautiful gift from God, and that I'm a good little girl. She would watch my favorite TV show with me, she would walk in the woods with me, she would talk to me, look at me, and she would say I want to know you, all about you. What do you like and dislike? She would rub my head and fall asleep with me, and hold me." (I visualized doing these soothing things with my beloved CS.)

Then my AS spoke lovingly to her. My AS invited her to sit in a sling I imagined I was wearing for her to snuggle with me all day. She looked so happy. Her eyes filled with love. When she was telling my AS about what she wanted Mommy to do for her, my AS felt a profound loneliness. Like a gaping hole or void of never-ending nothingness within me. (That must be the void I had talked about.) So much pain. I couldn't believe I could live with and function for so long with all that pain. I was slowly watching my deadened, hopelessly lonely baby and child selves come back to life through loving ICW, and it was such a gift.

Around the same time, my therapist talked to me about how my family didn't know how to be a family. She also pointed out how I couldn't get my parents' attention by being myself. I had to be what they wanted or be sick in order to get attention from them. The main times I got my father's attention were when I joined him in jobs he was doing around the house, or in my teens and twenties, when we went out to eat and drink together. I have some wonderful memories, though, of him playing in the water with my sisters and me on family vacations or taking us on motor scooters and snowmobiles at our second home when we were little. When he was present with us, it was wonderful. At times of sickness, I felt my mother's presence and attention most, and I cherish those memories.

I learned that it's important to remember that even when a child doesn't securely attach to their parents as a baby, there's still hope. It isn't a done deal, and it can be worked on later in life with the parents or through one's AS re-parenting their CS. However, when a child isn't emotionally attached to his/her parent(s), it's damaging, creates deep pain, and needs to be worked through in order to heal and have peace. Until some healing progress occurs, negative coping behaviors, like unhealthy self-medicating and codependency, take the front seat and create problems. The CS runs the show when the AS should be in charge.

* * *

I was seeing improvement in myself with all the ICW I was doing and continued this effort with the following journal entry describing God comforting me. I was in my bed saying a prayer I learned at church while experiencing considerable emotional pain, and it led to a healing vision:

> *"The light of God surrounds me. The love of God enfolds me. The power of God protects me. And the presence of God watches over me. Wherever I am, God is, and wherever God is, all is well."*
>
> *I could feel God enfolding me and suddenly saw my four-year-old self in God's hand, vomiting over and over. God wiped my little mouth, gave me water to rinse, and wiped my mouth again. God*

caressed my face and hair and told me He could see all of me. I got scared and thought, Oh no, He'll see I'm bad inside and be scared of me. But God didn't get scared, and He told me I was His child first and how He loved me so, every bit. Not good or bad, just me. He loved me unconditionally now and forever. My CS was shocked at first, then deeply touched, and then full of joy. My CS jumped up and down, hugging God and saying, "I really am okay. I'm okay. I'm lovable and good. I'm God's child."

I had a long road ahead of me to deal with my emotional pain. But, thankfully, I was slowly clearing some space by taking God's lead and *loving myself*.

There were many moments of emotional agony where I would call out to God for help or just vent my anger. He would somehow let me know over and over again that He loved me so, how I wouldn't get more than I could handle, and most importantly, that He would not forsake me. Sometimes God's messages were a stream of thought that just came to me. Other times a whole message would come all at once. It's hard to describe, and it was more like a sense of knowing.

One day while experiencing agonizing emotional pain and trying to get some relief by writing in my journal, I became aware of a stream of thought that God gave me. The feeling of coming unglued was unbearable sometimes, and it was at these times that I felt God's mercy. I wrote God's message in my journal, and I believe He says this to each of us when we open up to a presence of universal love:

"I am your mother and father at your core; this is so. I love you and cherish you. I hold you forever and always. You are my Divine child—a spiritual being. You are with me. See Me, feel Me, know that I am here for you. I love you with the greatest love."

Oh, that's so beautiful. I would hold onto those words like they were literally my lifeline and my only hope. I was so broken, and God held me up with His loving support. I would like to clarify that I refer to God as male only because that is historically how God is referenced in my spiritual tradition. I believe God is both mother and father, or that God is genderless. I also experienced moments where I wasn't so accepting of God's loving presence, as in my journal entry below.

> *I hear You, and I know it's true, but I'm blocking Your love. I'm so terribly scared, God. So, so scared! You say I'm safe; there is no safe. Stop trying to get me to buy into this. What if what you say isn't true? You are my last hope. If it's not true, I'll give up and die. What if my seeking was for nothing and there never will be any peace for me?*
>
> *I want to move on. Damn it, I'm sick of being sick, disconnected, and terrified. I'm fed up with all the work of hiding my symptoms. Can't I just fall apart and give up? I'm so damn tired of fighting for my life, fighting to heal. Too tired to go on.*

I continued to move in and out of extremely tormented states of depression, as noted in the following journal entry. These mood states would get triggered by a variety of situations and sometimes appeared to come out of nowhere. On one of my clinically depressed days, I was in bed again, feeling a very troubling degree of emotional pain throughout every fiber of my being.

Depression I

Well, guess what? My big two days of emotional reprieve came to a screeching halt. I need peace—please give me peace. I feel so heavy that trying to smile at my child, or play, or do any housekeeping seems far too great a task for me. I just want to crumble—to let go—to not have to be strong anymore. I want to stuff myself with food, to lie in bed, and sleep and cry in the darkness. This place is so dark—a hopeless, giving up place—a place where I fantasize about what it would be like to die, to just let go and slip away. I don't really want to die, but I do need help, God. I felt so good the last two days. I wanted to play, to be productive. I felt light—not anxious. Then I was hit with this depression so soon. It just makes me want to give up. It makes me question why I try, why I'm abstinent from alcohol and compulsive eating, why I bother with therapy and OA meetings. I want to be rid of this pain so badly. This depressive pain is worse than any physical pain I have experienced. It is **unrelenting, without conscience, brutal, and merciless**. *Will I ever heal? Will I? I'm mad, God. I try to be a good person. I work so hard at becoming whole. Is there hope for me?*

Can you relate to these thoughts and feelings? I hope not. But I'm guessing if you're a childhood trauma survivor, you probably do. Please take a moment and check in with yourself to see if you need to breathe, make sure you aren't taking on my pain, ground yourself in the present moment, and reassure yourself. You've got this. I know you can learn how to show up for yourself and help yourself through your difficult moments.

The poem below came to me after I wrote the above journal entry, and it romanticizes death as an escape from pain. Thank God I didn't go that route. Suicide was never the answer, but healing was. I have not known of a person who came out of the bowels of depression and still wished they had killed themselves. I've spoken to, heard of, and read about clinically depressed individuals who were grateful they didn't take their own life and how thankful they were to be alive *when they emerged from a depressive episode,* just like I did. It's important to remember how finding hope again after feeling so hopeless *is possible*.

The Release

O sweet death
As you cover me in your darkness
You shield me from my pain
From the endless work

You carry me off to nothingness
Without feeling
Just numbness

O blessed death
Carry me away on your black horse
Release me from my inner torment
And let me linger on a cloud of peace
Forevermore

****

This poem expresses my exhaustion with my inner battle and how I just wanted to be *released* from torment. Truthfully, though, I know that my depressed mind was lying to me by telling me death was a release. A release from what? Hell no, I'm not giving up! I'm dealing with my torment in this life once and for all.

My journals during this period continued to be full of consuming pain. It amazes me how effective my mind was at keeping my memories from me, but it sure didn't keep the emotional pain away. On the plus side, however, I wasn't *ready* to remember yet. I took antidepressants on and off for ten years when I needed extra support with my mood and would let the medication go once I felt stabilized using my coping toolbox.

With each welling up of old despair and pain, my anger would come out. Anger was the hardest to deal with. When I acted angrily with others, which usually took the form of irritability, it was a muted reflection of my inner discomfort. On a scale of 1 to 10, with 10 being the worst, if someone perceived me to be acting badly at a level 3 or 4, I was really at a 9 or 10 inner level of emotional distress. A level 3 with others was when I would overreact with curt responses and a generally bitchy tone, but the 9 or 10 within me felt like I was being internally abused. It even felt violent at times, like my insides were being stabbed or torn apart. Oh my gosh, can you relate to the torment being described here? My heart goes out to you and your pain.

It was exhausting having to hide my pain from others.

The resulting guilt and shame over being angry with those I love was another level of torment. If you're suffering internally, you know how hard it is to feel and act like a loving person. I tried with all my might to control it and express as little as I could with my loved ones. When I see someone acting badly now, I generally don't jump to thinking, *What a jerk,* or *What a horrible mother*. I pray for that person, because I know there is likely something negative driving their behavior. I hope for them to be given the support they need and find love and patience for themselves and their loved ones, instead of receiving more judgment from me.

If we could look into each other's hearts and understand the unique challenges each of us faces, I think we would treat each other much more gently, with more love, patience, tolerance, and care.
—Marvin J. Ashton[7]

As I recognized how dealing with my inner torment was consuming me, I also realized how it affected my ability to function. For a long time, I was perplexed by how I saw other mothers handle so much. Why couldn't I keep up? Well, when your cup is full of inner chaos, anxiety, and pain, how could there be much energy left? Considering what I was dealing with, I'm so proud of how well I held up and how my courage continued to move me forward with the faith that someday I would have peace. Thank God I had support and continued to work through my issues. I know how critical the support that God, my husband, family, friends, and professionals was in holding me up while I was doing some of the hardest healing work there is to do—trauma work.

* * *

As a result of my continued work on myself through therapy, there were some new skills on the horizon that I started to learn that helped me cope with my anger. I began setting healthy limits and standing up for myself; I learned not to overdo it and to take my needs into consideration, which then led to less anger. This process assists with

7 "Marvin J. Ashton Quotes," goodreads, accessed January 10, 2018, https://www.goodreads.com/quotes/51853-if-we-could-look-into-each-other-s-hearts-and-understand.

boundary work and lessening habitual codependent behaviors. Always focusing on other and putting them first is an act of abandoning self, and it fosters more anger. So, instead of saying "yes" right off the bat, I set a rule with myself: Marie, you have to say "No" or "I'll think about it" and sleep on it before you answer. I learned I am worthy enough to be considered first.

One aspect of boundary work I had begun was standing up for myself. For example, I pointed out to my husband how I didn't get birthday presents one year. He probably thought taking me out to dinner was my gift. Both he and my son always got presents on their birthdays, though, and I felt I should too. Not getting a present didn't feel good, and however juvenile it might have seemed, I needed to accept my feelings and stick up for myself by having my birthday acknowledged with a gift. It was scary to have that conversation, but empowering when I did, and my loving husband understood.

I started small and worked myself up in bigger ways, like saying no to others' requests. As I got better at it, the whole gift thing lost its power and wasn't as important. I was growing up. Since parts of me got developmentally arrested at the points of trauma and my self-medicating, I had some growing up to do. My arrested areas stemmed from my baby stage, four years old, and the adolescent/ teen years; they existed in parts of my personality. I also had other parts of myself that were very mature for my age. It was perplexing!

* * *

Another sign of growth was that I was becoming more aware of my anxiety. I thought everyone felt like that. Wasn't that the norm? But after trying a medication that quieted my anxiety, I thought, *Oh my gosh, is this what most people are feeling? No wonder they can do more.*

I think my anxiety primarily stemmed from my lack of trust in myself and the world. There didn't seem to be a safe zone other than with God, and I was shocked at how uncomfortable I was in my own skin. On the night of a party, I tuned into myself in a quiet moment and was taken aback by how uncomfortable and uncertain I felt. Did I even know who I was? Was I so used to playing the "I'm okay" game that I had completely lost my authentic self? I would question my social anxiety and think, *Am I good enough? Will I be approved of, or will I be judged, rejected, and abandoned?*

These thoughts were irrational, because I was liked and treated kindly, so where were they coming from? I think this came from deeper old emotions of not being good enough and feeling damaged, but not consciously knowing what that damage was. So I did what I could to cope during the social events. I distracted myself with food and alcohol to numb my anxiety.

I would think I must always be on guard for a possible attack. Who knows when someone might hurt me? Isn't that what people do? Then I would think to myself, *Why am I worried about an attack? That's never happened to me before.* Yes, repression is a very powerful thing, and I still couldn't remember.

Throughout the process of finding myself and learning how to "feel" my feelings, I blamed all my pain on my mother, because I still didn't know the truth about my childhood, and I needed a place to put the blame. Deep down inside, children blame themselves for their abuse, and my self-blame was totally hidden, like the memories. Once I got to the truth, I was able to move responsibility where it belonged instead of putting it all on my mother.

* * *

Note: Please take this in. I want to talk to you about choices you have on your own journey. I hope you can find a way to trust your inner knowing of what to do and how far to go into what you're working on. You may choose not to go so deep into ICW or your rage, and that's okay. You know best when it comes to what will help you and how much you can take at any given time.

If you can hold onto faith in God or the universe supporting you, you will see that things will occur synchronistically at the right time in your life. Experiences and people will show up to support you in ways you couldn't have planned for yourself, but you need to be open to that support in order to take advantage of it.

When problems hit or emotions run high, the child self tends to come to the surface. At these times, I believe you will get the best results by giving yourself extra tender loving care and patience, along with watching your thoughts. If your thoughts are self-critical, you can address them. For example, if you hear yourself say, "You are bad and will never be anything," you can speak the truth to yourself: "No, that's a lie! I'm doing the best I can, and that's good enough! I will be kind to myself because that's what I deserve." If you're acting up and feeling upset or experiencing a big emotional event, you can talk to your younger self. Just close your eyes and call to your CS. Comfort and reassure him or her; you will experience much better results than by being hard on yourself.

Whatever awful things you think you have done and deserve to be punished for, please let them go. Choose to give yourself the gift of strength and love by forgiving yourself instead. I do know that attacking ourselves causes our inner torment and behavior to worsen. It weakens us. Please, give yourself a break, forgive yourself, and be kind to you. I'll bet you will be pleasantly surprised at how you can turn yourself around. Also, consider finding a therapist you feel comfortable with to help you through your difficult healing work and the painful mental states that can occur on your journey. May you be blessed with healing peace.

Begin with a commitment to be kind to yourself
—Marianne Williamson[8]

8 Williamson, *A Course in Weight Loss*, 19.

Truth Slowly Bubbling Up

Trauma Memories

(37–43 years old)

It's hard to believe that after working with therapists on and off for nine years, I still didn't feel safe and strong enough to allow my repressed memories to surface. But now I know it wasn't time yet. I needed more in place before I was ready to remember. During my late thirties into early forties, my mind was giving me hints and preparing me for the truth—like the dream below.

Prior to having this dream, I had been told by a psychic that I had a family secret that involved deception and male influences. She refused to tell me what it was about, which made me angry. When it's bad news, it's common for psychics to withhold information. They feel it's unethical to just blurt it out, and they're probably right. Anyway, I was perplexed by this mystery, and as I was falling asleep that night, I asked my mind to help me dream about what the family secret was. Then I had this dream:

Dark Deception

I am digging in the dirt, and someone is telling me I'm deceiving myself. I think the deceit is helping me, but instead it's damaging. A man drives by all bloody and wounded. He leaves his car and runs. I direct a group of detectives after him. There is a woman in charge giving ridiculous and sexist reasons why I, who am the other female detective, should go after the wounded guy on my own and deal with him myself. I respond in a childlike voice, "I don't have to if I don't want to, right?" The woman in charge agrees, but she is manipulating me. It seems like a death mission because it's dangerous for me to go after him alone. Then the dream shifts to me being in a bathroom unable to relieve myself.

Wasn't that a telling dream? Too bad at the time I had no clue how to interpret it; rather, I just had that same old sneaking suspicion that something happened that I couldn't remember. When I did remember years later, I realized I could interpret the dream. First of all, digging in the dirt can be a metaphor for digging into one's dark or negative past. My mind was deceiving me by repressing the rapes I experienced as a survival mechanism. It was also damaging because I needed to know the truth in order to heal. I believe the bloody man represented the rapists having blood on their hands, meaning they were guilty.

I think rapists, especially pedophiles, are deeply wounded themselves, hence the bloody man's woundedness. My directing the detectives was indicative of a crime and my desire to know what happened. The woman in charge represented a societal myth that the victim is to blame and should take care of it herself. She also represented my mother, whom I felt failed to help me. The childlike detective was my

CS, who believed going after the bloody man was very dangerous. And, lastly, the bathroom scene was an ongoing dream theme for many years; it symbolized my emotions and memories were repressed and I was unable to release them. So, the dream was pretty easy to interpret once I remembered my past, and I was struck by how it spoke to what the psychic had mentioned.

* * *

During this time when I was dealing with the chaos of my old issues, I also struggled with my need to be a perfect mom. I held myself hostage to my ideal vision of "the perfect mother" by creating an image that was impossible to achieve. I was going to do and be everything that my CS wished she had, plus everything I read about in parenting books. I used this model to beat myself up for five years.

If I yelled, I would feel ashamed and go right to a black-and-white place of believing I was not a good mom, not a good person, or just not enough—period. My loving husband would try to reassure me that I was a good mother. I know that now, but I couldn't hear it then—I was too busy being my own judge and jury. Do you have an inner critic that waits for all the perfect moments to pounce and devour you in your time of vulnerability? It took years, but I eventually realized my inner critic was my ADS trying to defend and protect herself from a damaged adolescent's prospective. This part of myself needed to be loved, not told to go away. Once she felt safe, she quieted down.

I learned how feeding into this self-critical behavior, instead of reaching a metaphorical hand out to myself, just made me feel worse. If I had supported myself lovingly, I would have experienced the strength and positive behaviors that come from love, instead of the weakness that comes from criticism and fear. But it took time to learn a more positive way to relate to myself. Self-love isn't something most of us can learn overnight.

I started to realize how much I needed a break. My therapist, Georgette, told me repeatedly to find a way to take time for self-care. That was part of learning how to love myself. I had this idea that I should be with my child 24/7 and love every minute of it. I didn't hold a place for having my own needs, and I eventually learned that wanting time away or breaks from mothering did not make me a horrible person. I saw how demanding, difficult, irritating, and yet how full and wonderful mothering can be. Motherhood taught me incredible lessons about love and life. I was starting to wake up and see the whole picture—black, white, and that lovely gray area. This was another sign of progress where immature or arrested parts were growing up and forming a more mature outlook on life. Mommy breaks were, in fact, a blessing for both my child and me.

I mentioned earlier that I used perfectionism to compensate for feeling bad about myself and as part of my codependent behaviors (see Appendix E). While attending Overeaters Anonymous (OA), I realized that one of the ways my perfectionism played out was when I fell off the healthy-eating wagon. When I was not being the perfect OA member, I would become extremely self-punishing.

The structure of OA was good in many ways, but using it as another tool to whip myself was destructive. My relationship with food was another destructive act of self-hatred. The only solution or medicine that would bring lasting healing was self-love. When I recognized my harshness with myself, I would pray for help to be kind, asking, "How can I love myself?"

> *What is the most loving thing I could do for myself? What is the most loving way I could treat myself? Listen to the response of your heart and follow its guidance.*
>
> —Deepak Chopra and Oprah Winfrey[9]

* * *

During these years, the healing work continued, and at times, I became aware of a fierce storm raging within me. When I was thirty-seven, I drew a picture called *The Storm.* I was drawing with my son, and *The Storm* appeared. It was tightly held down, confined and restrained. Like in the picture with the symbolic expression coming from my mouth with its red eyes, it felt dark and sinister. The powerful image of *The Storm* picture profoundly captured what I sensed within myself. I just couldn't figure out what it was and why it was with me. It would be six more years before I had any idea that the storm was my hidden trauma.

9 Deepak Chopra and Oprah Winfrey, *21-Day Meditation Challenge, Miraculous Relationships*, 6 CD Set (Chopra Center, 2013).

The Storm

One day after drawing *The Storm*, I binged on food. I believe I unconsciously did this to push down the repressed memories that were trying to come up. I couldn't pretend eating was like going to the candy shop anymore. I couldn't find joy in it; only the self-punishing and numbing pieces were evident at this point. Food was such a complex issue because I used it to nourish, numb, and punish, and I used the fat it created as armor.

Food became an addiction, which created a disconnection between God and me, as well as between myself and the world, and it put me in a foggy state. It felt like I was stuck in a jail and the more food I ate, the emptier I felt. I couldn't understand why I engaged in this destructive and repulsive behavior. I would try to be patient and loving with myself, but it seemed too hard, so I just ate more.

Years later, after I'd made great strides in my healing journey, I looked back on my dreams, remembering all those visions of huge buffets and how I would eat endlessly. I haven't had a food dream in so long—I can't remember the last time I did. When a person's dreams shift to a healthier place, it's a telltale sign that healing is being internalized. It's a very positive indication of growth!

I believe my learning how to feel my feelings and care for my child and adult needs is what helped me let the food gorging go. I learned it was okay to be sad or mad and how to express those feelings with acceptance. They didn't hurt me, and I could express them on paper, speak them, sit quietly with them, or act them out. Being sad or mad was okay.

A short while after drawing *The Storm*, *The Gold* poem and pictures came. The storm, which symbolized my hidden traumas, had to be released before the gold (healing) could show itself. I believe they were both metaphors for the crisis phase of remembering that was on its way. I just knew these drawings were foretelling something intense to come.

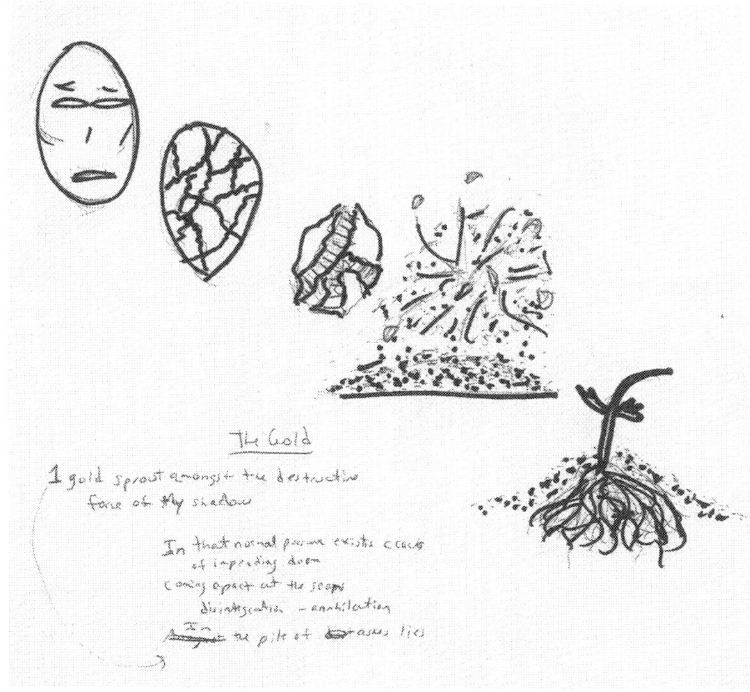

The Gold

In that normal persona exists cracks
Of impending doom
Coming apart at the seams
Disintegration—Annihilation
In the pile of ashes lies
One gold sprout among the destructive
Force of my shadow

****

Every time I look at *The Gold* drawing, I respond on a visceral level. It just speaks to my soul. *The Gold* poem describes the phases of *The Gold* drawing. The impending doom was the remembering. When I remembered, it felt like I was cracking then coming apart at the seams; finally, parts of me disintegrated and died. A sprout did appear in the ashes. That sprout was a rebirth of truth and resolution, which led to forgiveness, courage, passion, and peace. That sprout was, and always will be, pure gold to me. My hope is for you to *find your gold sprout and to nourish it.*

My inner struggles and chaos—along with my learning disabilities, like dyslexia, which I'll talk about later in the book—exhausted me. I wrote a poem about what a relief sleep was. Can you identify with the profound exhaustion caused by holding the damage of childhood trauma? I called my bed my great escape where I could finally get a break, as long as the nightmares weren't with me. Some of you may have experienced your traumas in your beds, and that may prevent your bed from being any kind of escape. I'm sorry for that, and I hope you have a place where you can feel comforted. Does the following poem remind you of dissociating (Appendix E, Glossary of Terms) or feeling detached from yourself? It sure does to me.

Dark Dream

I am low and tired
I am quiet and slow
There seems to be so little light
My light gets dimmer and dimmer
I want to hide
I want to collapse
Into a dream state of feeling detached
Far, far away I go
Into the darkest night
Off in the air on the wings of a dream
I am free from self—no more pain here for me

Sleep helped, but therapy was much more effective. My Jungian therapist, Georgette, pointed out that when I got emotional, it automatically led to chaos, and that was exhausting. Therapy played a key role in helping me name and sort through the chaos, so I could clarify and express feelings, which led to a calmer state.

Another piece of my inner chaos was that drama felt familiar and normal. It was hard for me to trust, which included trusting feeling good. Anxiety would ride on the tail of good feelings. This would then lead me to unknowingly seek out conflict in order to have an appropriate place to put my anxiety, tension, and fear. I needed to put that emotional energy somewhere, so I naturally gravitated to conflict or drama.

When I was a child, there was so much hype around everything being perfect, but underneath was anxiety and pain. This was confusing and led me to distrust when things *appeared* good. I tried to flow with the good feelings, since my family, friends, and neighbors were acting as if life was great when I was a child, but at the same time, I would question, "Really, this is great?" The happy childhood experiences coupled with hidden trauma pain made me feel confused.

At thirty-eight, I wrote this journal entry about letting go of conflict and chaos:

> *Today in the here and now, I know the sham is up. Things really are good and not loaded with tension unless I put it there. I can trust that I'm doing well, and that feeling okay is safe. I don't need to create conflict. I really can have peace in my life, and I deserve peace. My loving husband and child and I are doing well and without a hidden agenda. I'm thankful to be learning this.*

I was relieved to see myself becoming aware of my unhealthy need for the familiarity of chaos and working toward learning how to sit with comfort, peace, and good times. It took a lot of practice!

* * *

I want to share with you a happy story about birthing my daughter when I was thirty-eight. My husband and I had been trying to conceive for three and a half years and after several miscarriages, were finally having our little girl. Since my son's birth was difficult, my husband agreed to take a HypnoBirthing course with me. The fear of another birthing trauma reawakening my PTSD filled me with anxiety. The class was exactly what I needed and greatly reduced the anxiety. One of my dear friends, Jessica, who is both a midwife and doula, helped us with the birth. We had a beautiful and empowering water birth without drugs and had success with breastfeeding. I was so happy!

The whole experience was healing, and I will never forget the look on my husband's and son's faces when they saw our baby girl for the first time. My husband got to cut the cord, and I finally got to see my baby's sweet, loving face. I didn't struggle after her birth in the way that I did after my son's delivery, because my PTSD wasn't triggered. What a totally different outcome when I was okay and functioning. It was another sign of progress. I advocated for myself by taking the class and practicing the program throughout my pregnancy, which de-escalated my anxiety. A tension-filled, frightened mom doesn't usually have a graceful birth, so I worked with myself daily by walking, doing yoga, and listening to the affirming HypnoBirthing CDs while resting; I did all I could to train my mind to calm down.

Right before the birth, I felt the power of nature was helping us, and I wrote this poem:

Horse Goddess

Going with the primal birthing force
Is like riding the white goddess horse.
She carries me
Her power holds and protects me.
I bloom like a rose awakening
To see my infant Safe and Free
And I trust nature's force.
A power that is new to me.
A power that does not annihilate.

****

After my baby girl's birth, God sent me an angel friend named Yoko. She lived near me and, later, with my family for a while. She was comforting, gentle, sincere, loving, and supportive. I will always hold her kindness in my heart. Upon waking, Yoko's loving face was there, asking me, "What can I do for you today?" She taught me beautiful lessons about how to be present and loving with others.

I was a happy mommy with periodic depressive episodes that would rear their ugly heads. My well of sadness would become disabling and even life-threatening at times. Can you identify with the following peek into my seriously depressed mind? If you're a survivor, I'll bet you will be intimately familiar with the deep pain of depression. Here is a journal entry describing one of my clinical depressions from when I was forty.

Depression II

Sadness, darkness, hiding, crawling, lingering, waiting, shutting down, watching, immobile, unclear, lost. No thinking, no action, just sitting, lying, sleeping, numbness. **Shame**, *so much shame, failure, not good enough, staring but not seeing, heavy, sick, sore, unable to tolerate stimulation like people's voices or even their energy, others' needs, chores, even self-care all too much.*

A blanket resting over me, smothering me. Where am I? I am lost wandering aimlessly; hide, distract, incapable, wet rag, resentment, discouragement, why bother. Christopher Reeve said something about taking action before depression's grip gets you. But when you're this low, there's no energy for action. It takes all my strength to lift my arm. There is no desire to move, just for release from this tormented place. I want to give up, it's hopeless. I'M UN-HELPABLE.

If I'm sick enough, I won't have to do anything—you can all go away now—Leave me alone! I'm sick of everyone and everything coming at me every waking moment. I'm not what you think. I'm small and sick and vulnerable and oh so tired, so fragile.

A thread hanging on by a thread. Don't let go or you will fall into the void where you'll never be found again—where people's minds go and they don't come back. You're lost forever until that final moment of release where there is no more work, no more expectation, no endless inner torment.

* * *

Remember, as long as you are breathing
it's never too late to start a new beginning.
—Robert Tew[10]

During this time, I had a very distinct fear of getting too close to my devastation because I was afraid I would go too far and be unable to recover (i.e., just completely lose my mind and be in a totally weakened state). I realized after many visits to my edge of darkness that *my fear of being unable to return was one of many lies my mind told me.* This misbelief kept me from going where I needed to go so I could continue to heal. Each and every fear I faced was scary, but I felt like I got the help I needed or received God's grace, and that led to feeling relief. My fear-based mind wanted to keep me afraid and in the dark so that I wouldn't face myself and heal. What I needed to do was address my fear while accepting God's reminders that I never deal with my fear alone when I allow His supportive love to carry me through. In that act of opening myself up to Divine Power, I'm supported and healing. I never do anything alone. Either I do it with God and gain strength, or I choose fear and become weaker.

Your suffering does not make you weak;
only your avoidance of suffering makes you weak.
—Marianne Williamson[11]

It's hard to believe how deep in the well of depression I would sink, but thankfully, I would reemerge with hope for better days. A few years after the crisis phase of remembering, I found I didn't go into these debilitating depressions anymore. Oh my dear God, I am

10 Robert Tew, "As Long as You Are Breathing," Live Life Happy, June 28, 2013, https://livelifehappy.com/.

11 Williamson, *A Course in Weight Loss*, 163.

so very grateful! I hope for all survivors, and anyone dealing with depression, to also experience the relief of sweet, peaceful healing, or at least to be released from the depths of depression.

* * *

At forty-one years old, I sensed something was trying to come up. I'd encountered a series of events that were taking me down—watching a movie about a child being abused and seeing another child sexual abuse article in the local newspaper. It was one thing after another; on the surface, they seemed like mere coincidence, but I believed they were synchronistic. I thought God was helping me face what I needed to face. Those experiences sent me into a terrible state. I felt taken down, frightened, and shaky, and I "checked-out" into "spaciness." This experience is an example of being triggered, leading to the spacey, dissociated feeling.

At times, I felt as if a ball or mass was physically trying to come up into my chest and throat. It felt old, like it had been with me forever. I just stared straight ahead, like I was a million miles away and obsessed for days about the upsetting things I'd seen or read. Sometimes, I spontaneously started to shake days after seeing a television show or reading an article. Exposure to other children's sexual abuse stories made me feel like they had a grip on me that I couldn't shake. I found myself standing transfixed, staring at the TV, feeling like I couldn't move while a survivor on a show talked about his or her abuse. It was intense and odd, and it scared me. I didn't know what to make of it. But I did know it meant something important. Most people don't respond like that; there must have been a reason for it.

At those times, thoughts would flash through my mind, like

remembering the time the psychic told me there was a dark secret involving a malebehaviors. I would later have rape dreams and wake up feeling victimized, deeply saddened, and abandoned. I did have a sense that God was trying to help me remember, but I didn't have any specifics. What happened and with whom? One would think the dreams would have answered my questions, but I couldn't see it or put it together. I would write journal entries listing facts that pointed to there being something about sexual abuse, but I just couldn't reach that conclusion yet. It seemed an impossible thing to have happened to me. I was still blocking my ability to remember by unconsciously repressing my memories. I wish I could have trusted that I would remember when the time was right—when I felt safe and strong enough and had the necessary support system in place.

* * *

One of my supporters was an alternative practitioner, who was an ex-monk named Jack. Several bruises mysteriously appeared on my lower abdomen during treatment. This practitioner used herbal patches and energy work to help me with my emotional and physical state, and he never even touched my lower abdomen. I believe my body was releasing trauma and providing another sign to keep searching for the truth behind the mysterious bruises.

I decided to study energy treatments, spiritual teachings, and Chi Gong practices with Jack and his wife. After telling them about one of my dreams, in which I had been attacked and felt sick and emotionally distressed afterward, he told me I had trauma in my past that needed to be unblocked. He said it was causing disease in my body. So he taught me a meditative practice that would protect me spiritually and help me to remember my past without feeling victimized again.

I was reluctant at first, but he and his wife supported me and helped me remember, and I am very grateful to them.

The first time I tried the meditation, I recovered a memory of myself at my childhood home. In the memory, I was alone in my bedroom and saw a picture I had drawn as a teenager while I was high. It was a picture of me pointing a gun at my head and pulling the trigger, with blood flowing out.

I also remembered waking up the next day as a teen, shocked by that drawing. I was cut off or compartmentalized from those disturbing feelings and genuinely confused by them. Therefore, I hid the drawing under my mattress. It's a perfect metaphor—just like I hid or repressed my trauma memories, wanting to die deep in my mind! I had completely forgotten this memory for years. After the memory came, I searched through my old drawing pad from my teen years, and there it was. This helped me trust the memory process I was currently using because I actually held in my hands the physical picture, which I had forgotten existed.

* * *

Note: I'm going to be moving into various other spiritual experiences I had that seemed really unusual to me. Then again, spiritual or healing journeys are unique to each of us. The experiences I refer to throughout this book could be called visions. My visions occurred when I was awake, and I had control over them; I could just let them flow, or I could stop if I wanted. In my personal experience, I found they automatically came at quiet times, almost like watching a movie. These visual experiences were an instrumental piece of my healing process. It doesn't matter what I call them or even what they were specifically about. What mattered was they provided me with insight and were a gauge of my progress; they comforted me and gave me faith to keep striving to heal. *The important thing to remember is for us to utilize our strengths and recognize what feels supportive in our efforts to keep our healing moving forward.*

I will speak often of spiritual experiences, and I hope you can filter out any language you're uncomfortable with. If you're feeling far from God, please don't worry—you can reach God in your own unique way, when and if you choose to. God will work with you and connect with you in a form you understand and feel comfortable with. It doesn't have to be a vision of Jesus or a spiritual being. Your connection with God could be a deep feeling of love you experience walking in the woods, a loving thought, or a kind gesture from another person. The possibilities are endless!

It's your choice to allow yourself to open up to the Divine in your life when and if you're ready. Just remember that God will show up in a form you can embrace and feel safe around, and that Divine Presence can be your most profound comfort, your most powerful healer. For many of us, the desperation of deep suffering has a way of being the critical vehicle we need to allow ourselves to open our hearts to the Divine Presence of God. In other words, hitting bottom has a way of cracking one open to receive in desperation.

The other spiritual piece I want to mention is that many Holy Beings—such as Jesus, the Virgin Mary, and various Eastern religious figures—would appear to me in my mind during the visions. I can feel some of you cringing at this point, but please hang in there. Who was appearing wasn't important. To me, all the Holy Ones were different representations of the Holy Spirit or God.

Their presence in my mind was paramount in helping me feel supported and safe enough to continue to remember and keep going. I felt so alone and abandoned that I needed an army of spiritual support in order to go on. Remember, you always have the option to take from my experience what feels supportive to you, and if it doesn't, just let it go. So, take what you're comfortable with and leave the rest.

Please don't think you need to have similar mystical experiences in order to heal. Each of us finds healing in our own unique way. I pray you allow your authentic healing process to emerge within you.

* * *

I had a vision when I was forty-three related to the section of my spine called the T6 and T7 region. I had been going for regular treatments with my alternative practitioner, Jack. At each appointment, we would discuss how energetically blocked the T6 and T7 vertebrae on my spine were and how this was an indication of emotional issues. I was encouraged to do prayer mat work in order to find out what I was hiding from myself.

I was also instructed to take detox baths with baking soda, hydrogen peroxide, and Epsom salts to pull out toxins as part of my healing work. During one of my baths, I had a vision symbolizing progress with energetic work with my body.

Energy Bundle Vision

> *A Holy One is showing me an energetic bundle or mass around my T6 and T7 vertebrae. I see energy as colors moving up and down the bundle. The mass is dark and looks disgusting. Oh my gosh, the Holy One is bending down and ripping it off with such force; then he flings it into a fire. Those vertebrae now look like a raw, open wound, and the Holy One is taking light from himself and reaching inside me to engulf my wound in light and wrapping it up with bandages. He tells me to rest. I'm grateful because I think I'm one step closer to remembering. I'm getting help unblocking this area of my body, and I can feel the truth getting closer.*

I tried to stay open-minded during these experiences because intuitively I knew I was being helped, and it didn't matter if I understood what was happening. I didn't feel afraid, so I just surrendered to the process.

For times when I was in crises and feeling emotionally taken down, Jack told me to try shock therapy for my intense moods, which involved submerging myself in cold water baths for twenty minutes. Let me tell you, it was a shock all right, but it definitely helped. That cold water knocked my brain onto another track.

One of the spiritual practices Jack was teaching a group of students was how to read incense ashes. I had heard of reading tea leaves, but incense was a new one for me. All the intricate shapes the incense burnings would create were interesting and surprising. I would regularly burn incense at my home altar with a specific intention and then draw a picture of the shape of the ashes in my journal to show Jack for interpretation. One design looked like a gate. Jack said,

"What door are you trying to open?" I know what door that was, and it was about to finally bust open!

About three months before my first trauma memory, one of my sisters sent me a note with words I had sent her years earlier during one of her serious depressive episodes. They were words that I would soon need but didn't know it at the time—another example of the synchronicity at work in my healing journey. These signs gave me hope.

> *"Thank you for showing us the courage to feel your feelings, to genuinely express where you're at, for showing us how to look the deepest darkness in the eye and come out on the other side, how you remind us how precious life is, no matter how hard it is and how there is joy even when things seem hopeless."*

Thank you, Sis. I needed to hear those words, and I read them many times when things got rough and I needed reassurance.

Children and teens commonly experience stomach problems as an expression of emotional distress they can't handle psychologically. I began to remember experiencing such problems. One night when I was forty-three years old, I asked myself to dream about why I'd had intense attacks of stomach distress when I was younger and why I still had current stomach issues. This dream was what came up.

My Teen's Empty House

I have to keep going to the bathroom. I find a door open, and I close it. I go to walk outside to a beach but find a flood. I am back in a house with a young teen girl. Her house is empty. Everything of value has been sneakily stolen from her. So much anguish, sorrow, mistrust, and abandonment. There is no one there for her. I, as an adult, am with her. I sob, aching and crying over and over at this teen's pain. I can't begin to take in the enormity of her suffering. The teen girl just stands there, numb and lifeless. She stares but doesn't see. There are people lurking in the background outside, looking to see if anything of value is left for them to sneak in and steal.

Wow, even when dreams are pretty clear, their meanings can be elusive when traumas are still repressed! I awoke with the teen's pain haunting me. I was in such a disturbed state after that dream and mystified by the degree of pain.

Only after I started remembering was I able to make sense of the empty house dream. My mind was slowly preparing me to face the atrocious events of my past. The teen girl was me. I had so much pain to release in the bathroom, which was a metaphor for releasing my repressed traumatic feelings. When I saw that the door to trauma was open, I closed it because I wasn't ready to remember. When I went out to the ocean of emotion, there was a flood of feelings and memories that were too much for me. The teen girl's house was empty because she felt empty, and the rapists sneakily robbed her of her self-value, her innocence, and her trust in the world. She forever felt unsafe and haunted by the people lurking outside. My teen self was alone with her pain, and she dealt with it by keeping herself numb and dissociated by self-medicating with alcohol and drugs. My AS was able to feel the pain, and it was *staggering*.

But how long could I hold all that pain inside? I know there were signs that something was amiss, but I camouflaged and misinterpreted them in order to protect myself.

Remembering was so close, and I was ready! All the years of therapy strengthened me, and I had all kinds of support around me. Most of all, my powerful spiritual connection was in place. I was going to need every bit of help to withstand what I was about to endure. I was entering the crisis phase of remembering. So put on your seatbelt, because this was two years of raw positive and negative intensity, plus incredible growth and healing.

In the Darkest Crevices I Roam

Crisis Phase

(43–45 years old)

PART I

The First Memories

And the day came when the risk to remain tight in a bud was more painful than the risk it took to blossom.

—Anaïs Nin[12]

And so, healing from my trauma began when I started to remember being raped. All the previous healing work I had done had been laying the foundation to prepare me for this crisis phase. It's called the *crisis phase* because the memories are as fresh and raw as the day the trauma or crisis occurred (see Appendix E, Glossary of Terms). They were just locked away and never dealt with until they resurfaced and stunned me.

I had been having nightmares about my rapes all my life but had discounted them every time. I had also been having mini-flashbacks. For example, when someone moved a certain way while standing over me, or I heard a particular sound, I would have an uncharacteristically panicked response. I became suspicious about my symptoms and had asked my therapist to hypnotize me fifteen years before I entered the crisis phase, but I could never seem to get to those appointments. I figured it wasn't time to get at whatever was haunting me then, but the time was now approaching.

---

12 "Anaïs Nin Quotes," goodreads, accessed January 11, 2018, https://www.goodreads.com/quotes/2846-and-the-day-came-when-the-risk-to-remain-tight.

After seeing the incense ash reading I mentioned earlier, I won a free hypnotherapy session. Synchronicity at its best! During the free hypnotherapy session, I was guided into a deep hypnotic state. I became aware of a symbolic and foreboding female face at my third eye (center forehead). The face was intense and powerful, and I sensed it was the mother/warrior I mentioned earlier. I also saw blood dripping from my third eye, and my shadow character said she was there to tell me my trauma story. The therapist asked me if I was ready to hear it, and I cried out "No! I'm so scared!" As soon as I said no, I was thrown out of my hypnotic state, fully awake. I knew I was close to the truth; I could feel it. I needed to get myself ready first, so I left the hypnotherapy session and prepared spiritually.

A week after that session, a child I knew—a four-year-old, the same age I was when I was first molested—was also molested, and the news was devastating. It brought up so much of my own pain, pain that felt really old. It felt like it had been with me forever. Do you know that feeling too? The news made me feel connected to something in my past.

When any pain, difficulty, frustration, or challenge emerges, try to see it, honor it, bear witness to it, and receive it as part of your healing.

—Marianne Williamson[13]

During my spiritual preparation for the second hypnotherapy session, I prayed for the Pure Light or Holy Ones to protect, comfort, and help me to remember. This was too big for me to do alone; I needed help. I was taking shock therapy baths, reasoning with myself that

13 Williamson, *A Course in Weight Loss*, 172.

I was stronger than my emotions, and reminding myself that what happened was in the past and it was safe now to remember.

The way I was able to feel safe enough was by getting very close to Holy Ones from the Catholic, Buddhist, and Hindu religions. So, before the next hypnosis, I meditated while taking a bath and asked to be spiritually comforted when the time came to remember. I asked Kwan Yin (the Goddess of Mercy) if I could look at her beautiful face because she calmed me. Then I had a vision in which she gave me a lotus flower, which passed through my chest wall and wrapped around my heart. She held another lotus flower at her heart, and light passed from her heart to mine. This experience made me feel peaceful and confident that remembering would be okay.

These visual experiences were powerful reminders that I was not alone with my fear and pain. My highly visual nature and open-mindedness was coming in handy as a healing tool. When it's time for you to remember, you will naturally be drawn to helping tools that work for you. Here's a journal entry about my therapy preparation.

> *There's that familiar sensation of a mass trying to come up in my upper abdomen and chest area again. I've moved into an angry and anxious state. I'll try to support myself by resting, praying, and giving myself reassurance, all of which help lessen my painful feelings. Okay, now I'm in a more saddened state and feel quiet and ready. I contact Jack's wife, Ellen, and she tells me I can ask the Holy Ones for help breaking the memory block during hypnosis. This is good news because I know that block has been impenetrable thus far.*

I went back for the second hypnosis session and settled into a comfortable recliner. I went under easily while sensing the Holy Ones with my mind's eye. At first, all I could see was a huge wall, so I asked for it to be broken. A Holy One had a long powerful stick and smashed the wall down the middle. Then the female mother/warrior named Kali came in and pulled each side back so I could see. I had part of one memory. The hypnotist saw me choking, violently flailing about, and making childish sounds of fear and struggle. He got scared and pulled me out of it. It was as though it was happening right in that moment with all the feeling and picture memories at once. It was terrifying to experience and, I assume, to witness.

I was furious with him! How dare he pull me out of my memory! I had waited for what felt like lifetimes to finally remember. Damn! I was mad, but I did understand since choking and thrashing about on his recliner wasn't okay either. The hypnotherapist pointed out how I appeared childlike and wished he had videotaped it so I could see it. I wished he had taped it too. A word of warning, though: it's important to have supporters like a therapist or extra help at home since suddenly remembering in hypnotherapy can put a person in a compromised state.

The next week was hell, pure hell. I was in deep emotional distress, and everywhere I turned, there were stories about child rape. If I turned on the TV, it was there. When I picked up the paper, there was an article on a pedophile computer sting. When I walked in while my husband was watching the news, I heard it there too. I went downstairs to exercise and watch TV, and a movie about a child being sexually abused was playing. I knew I was getting help to see the truth—no more *secrets*! It was time to remember.

After being exposed to child rape stories, I would go in and out of intense emotional states (trauma *triggers*) where I would shake and sob while simultaneously feeling sadness, confusion, rage, and nausea. At this point, I knew for sure that rape was what I was remembering. In the month following my second appointment, my deep rage toward the men who raped me was surfacing once again, but this time I knew why fury was with me. Here is an example from my journal:

RAGE II

YOU STOLE (rapist)—You took from me—you broke me—you stole my sweet innocence—smothered me with your evil rage and control.

You hurt, you destroyed, you annihilated MY HEART. I'm so lost in this pain, this death sentence you forced on me.

I want to gouge your eyes out.
I want to reach into your chest and rip your heart out, rip it to shreds and throw it on the dirty ground and pound it into nothingness, nonexistence.

I want to strangle you and watch you suffer.
I want to torture and torment you for all the days of your life.

The pain—the death—the void—the numbness—the dissociation you have caused with your acts of pure evil. Go to hell, you piece of shit, go to hell where you belong, tormented forever!

WOW, that really expressed my inner experience! After writing this, I allowed myself to let go of some more rage and express myself by acting out attacking the rapist, while at the same time letting out awful wailing sounds. Thankfully, I had time at home alone to do this disturbing yet healing release work. I was shocked at the degree of rage that was in me. I heard myself making sounds I didn't know I could make while I jabbed at a pillow or visualized striking out. I was amazed that I could have held this within me for so long without knowing. I intuitively knew it had to come out—not just the memory but all the collateral damage too!

The next remembering event was later that same month, and it spontaneously happened during a bath. As I soaked in the warm water, listening to it run out of the faucet while soft music played in the room, I saw the rape at my childhood home. It was the one that happened when I was nine or ten that I had nightmares about over the years. It was like watching a movie of my attack without any emotional or physical response—I felt neutral. I'm grateful to God for that. Right before I remembered, the Virgin Mary and Kwan Yin put a lotus flower over my heart and comforted me. After the memory surfaced, I journaled the following:

> *Hiding sounds really good. I feel small and sad—depressed—I really don't want to move. There is much to do, and I feel totally incapable. I want to curl up in a big lotus flower till my wounds heal.*

And then, this poem came:

THE LOTUS

Lotus flower so wide and open,
will you close around me and protect me,
hold me,
hold me till I have the strength to see?
Lotus flower,
let me rest in your beautifulness,
so soft and sweet,
protected, safe, and asleep,
Asleep till I can breathe and see
from your open bloom once again.

I'm grateful for the Virgin Mary and Kwan Yin and poems like this one that comforted me.

***

I want to share one final instance with you before I move on. I awoke in a hotel room my family and I were staying at on one of my husband's work trips in New Hampshire and journaled this dream.

> *What a long detailed dream about needing to birth a baby (trauma) while being in excruciating pain. My midwives were my friends who were going to cut me open and pull it out. There was a big build-up as it (remembering) got closer, and I drank lots of alcohol. I was trying to help myself tolerate the agony. I was cut open a bit (first couple of memories) and the rest would happen later. My loving husband was there supporting me. Different people in my support network would come and go to support in different ways. Even with all that help, I still felt so alone with my pain and far away from everyone.*

I would wake up from intense dreams like this one feeling sad, heavy, and exhausted. It had such an effect on me that I asked my family to go to dinner with friends without me that night. I needed to be alone. It was amazing how dreams just told me what I needed to know, and this dream described my remembering process. In my sleep, it was pointed out how I used alcohol to self-medicate and keep memories down. Alcohol abuse mirrored my dreams while I was awake. But this was another form of abuse I had to face and overcome if I was to continue my journey of healing.

PART II

AA and Flashbacks

I had started to drink a lot at night after the kids went to bed during the months leading up to the hypnotherapy. Some part of me was trying to keep the memories down. I was feeling stuck in a place of desperately wanting to know what felt so hidden yet terrified to know the truth.

I tried everything I could think of to stop drinking, but I just couldn't. I told myself not to drink at night and failed, limited the alcohol in the house and failed, got rid of the alcohol and went out for more and failed. I knew it was time to go to AA at that point. There would be no progress in recovering my memories and healing if I was actively numbing myself. I suspected the nighttime drinking would eventually spill over into the daytime with the kids, so I decided to go to AA for some support before things got out of control.

Going to AA was very difficult for me, but it was also a huge source of support and turned out to be exactly what I needed at that time. I was scared walking into those initial meetings, feeling full of shame but also relieved to be welcomed by the members. I learned to stop using alcohol to push away the memories and instead to let them come; I learned to surrender. About a week after I stopped drinking, the emotional pain escalated. I had also gotten an AA sponsor and was struggling to hang on to abstinence.

One day that first week, I was driving on a dirt road, and I received a phone call from my new AA sponsor. I'm not totally clear about our conversation except the part when she gave me an ultimatum about how I needed to do what she told me to do or she wouldn't sponsor me. Normally, this wouldn't have been a big deal, but at that time just after giving up my numbing alcohol and also experiencing my memories and pain trying to come up, I was a vulnerable open wound. I believe my child self was right on the surface and associated my sponsor's threat with the rapists' threats. You know the kind: "Do what I say, or I'll kill you," or "You tell anyone, and I'll come after you and your family."

Her words went through my trauma filter, and my whole body started shaking as I drove. I told her I had to go, pulled over, and dropped my phone in a state of panic. In that moment, I had my first uninterrupted full-blown flashback. This is the car flashback from the rape I shared with you in the trauma chapter.

My mind knew I couldn't handle the whole package of physical, emotional, and visual memories at once. Flashbacks generally had physical and emotional memories without mental pictures. Then the visual memory usually came at another time without the feeling part, which made it more tolerable for me to handle. In this flashback, I could feel intense emotion and physical sensations like clenching my teeth, making awful noises, and flailing about, but my mind was chaotic without discernable visual aspects of a memory. I was given bits and pieces of memories with time to process, and then given more. It was truly amazing and mind-boggling how the whole process played itself out; I was pushed to the brink of my breaking point many times then pulled back to recover my strength before remembering more.

Maybe terror and dread, once experienced, embed themselves into you. Even when the cause has gone, leaving behind a sleeping horror that is too easily awakened.
—Rosamund Lupton[14]

Because of all the healing work I'd done over the years, I was able to handle these shocking new revelations with grace and self-love instead of turning to substances to self-medicate. AA had helped me take that final step of turning away from alcohol as a negative coping behavior. Instead, I allowed the raw emotions to arise without censoring them. They didn't kill me; they helped me heal because they opened even more room for self-acceptance.

Still, that didn't mean this was easy. One particular day, I thought, *Go to God, then call your sponsor, and be kind to yourself.* My sponsor reassured me and suggested an AA meeting. Then I prayed and rested, while my kids where at school, and it helped for a while, but as night approached, the tension grew.

> **(SHIELDS UP)** *I go into my bedroom to pray and meditate, and as soon as I close my eyes, I see my teen self cutting herself all over her face, head, and front of her body. I see her covered in blood, and she's shaking all over and gasping for air. I see her mouth stuffed with something. Then she tells me she feels like a piece of shit, a piece of meat, worthless and abused and thrown out. Abandoned.* **(DEEP BREATH)**

14 Rosamund Lupton, *Sister* (New York: Crown, 2011), 32.

She didn't speak to me, but I knew what she was thinking. She was punishing herself. It was about her shame. It's difficult to describe what it's like seeing myself like this. It was so disturbing that it rattled me to my core. I have to say how sad it is to know that many abused children feel the same way about themselves deep inside. Being burdened with shame and self-loathing. Can you relate to this level of shame that breeds self-hatred and punishment?

Let's take a moment to check in so you can connect with yourself and take deep, calming breaths just to reset yourself in the present moment. You can also reassure your CS that you and your younger self are safe in this moment.

I was surprised by how clear these visual experiences were, and I knew they weren't happening at that moment but that they were part of my healing process. I prayed to Jesus, asking Him, "How can I help my teen self?" Then I had an ICW talk with my teen self about how it wasn't her fault, how the rapist had committed a crime, etc. She then asked me for drugs and said to leave her alone.

As I continued to talk lovingly to her, she started to cry, and I held her as she remembered one of her ADS's rapes. She shook, cried out, and experienced her horrific pain in my AS's loving arms. She had a witness, and for the first time, Teen Marie was not alone with her secrets.

Healing occurred, and I knew my AS had planted a seed in my teen self that she was not to blame, she was good, and she deserved loving-kindness instead of being cut up and punished. I was seeing firsthand the power of sitting with the truth, no matter how scary or dark it was. By allowing myself to express my hidden secrets, I was moving forward on my journey, and it didn't do more damage. I refused to turn away from my darkness, instead embracing my pain and myself with love the best I could. I knew that I must walk through fear if I wanted to heal. I must not ignore it or bury it under addictions and distractions, but instead look it in the eye and walk through my darkness into the Light.

> *The universe will never leave you alone at such a time as this. Angels are all around you, as they gather without fail whenever a soul is seeking its wholeness.*
>
> —Marianne Williamson[15]

The vision of my teen self cutting helped me understand one of the reasons why some people cut themselves. I was self-punishing since I felt I was bad, that I was to blame for what happened to me.

Note: Please take this in. If you experience self-blame, please know that it is *not true*. You are not to blame; you are good. Since children know someone is to blame but no one takes responsibility for abuse, the child takes it. You deserve nothing but loving-kindness and support to heal your wounds. Only love heals and makes you stronger; self-punishment just creates more fear and weakens you. Please find a way to give yourself love. *Your sexual abuse was not your choice, and it was not your fault!* Even if your abuser manipulated and brainwashed you or groomed you into believing you wanted to be abused or that it was your fault, please recognize that's not the truth. Your abuser chose to abuse you, not the other way around.

* * *

15 Williamson, *A Course in Weight Loss*, 172.

During this time, I continued going to AA meetings and abstaining from alcohol, although I was in and out of a lot of pain. I was forty-four years old at this point and had been dealing with flashbacks for eight months when one night at a women's AA meeting I discussed one of these episodes. Afterward, one of the women gave me the crisis hotline number for our local Sexual Assault Intervention Services and said I should consider calling because she thought I was having flashback memories. The next day, I had the worst flashback yet, so I called the hotline number for help while in a traumatized state. They had a counselor contact me in a few days.

I felt beaten down and so alone. I was a mess and needed support. I still don't know how I went on doing anything like driving my kids back and forth to school. In hindsight, that probably wasn't a good idea. I would do the absolute minimum—no dishes, very little cooking, no cleaning. I just felt so *overwhelmed*, drained, and exhausted.

My sister and brother survivors, I know you know what I'm talking about, that devastatingly drained feeling. Have you experienced it too?

The toll the crisis phase took on me was extensive. After flashback memories, I would feel detached from my body. I would stutter and have trouble forming thoughts and then speaking them. My short-term memory was nonexistent, and I would have trouble moving my body normally. I could sit in a chair and not move at all for periods of time, like I was far away. I was so, so tired. These symptoms would go on for days, and it would take up to two weeks to feel normal again. This would all fuel my drinking urges.

On one of my particularly brutal days, while waiting to hear back from the sexual assault services, this happened. There was that feeling of inner edginess where I didn't know what to do with my uneasiness and was struggling with drinking urges and wanting to crawl into a hole. I would think, *I'm just not fit to be around other humans.* Then I dropped to the floor once again with a full-on flashback flailing through the air and then had the following vision, which had a significant effect on me.

The Devil's Offer

There's a wall between God and me today. I stand in darkness—the dark one accompanies me and slithers like a snake between my feet trying to seduce me. He calls for me to give up the fight to heal and instead rest in addictive darkness with him—he said to let the dark horse carry and release me from my suffering. Then there was quiet. I STOMPED ON HIM AND YELLED "NOOOOOO! I WILL NOT FORSAKE MYSELF, YOU LYING, SLITHERING SNAKE! YOU SON OF A BITCH! GO BACK TO HELL WHERE YOU BELONG!"

Lies! There is no rest in the darkness of addiction. There is no relief from suffering, just deeper suffering and eventual death. All addictive roads lead to the end—death.

I have a choice, and I choose the Light. I choose to heal. I choose to rest in God's hand and accept His comfort during times when inner torment is ravishing my soul. God holds me up until I can hold myself up, and He reminds me of His love for me. He never forsakes me, and I won't forsake me.

I know I'm okay. I have a beautiful support system, I have a strong connection with God, I am aware of my needs, and I know how to reach out for help.

I will call my husband and then I'll call for professional help.

No matter how hard it is, I will move through it one step at a time. I'm strong, and I deserve to have peace and be okay. It won't stay this bad. Holding onto hope.

Can you relate to the above struggle with addiction and battling with it, or being enticed by sly, manipulative, addictive thoughts? This darkness is such a weight. Understanding this can help survivors of abuse to give themselves grace on their journey of healing. It's a lot to handle amid the daily responsibilities of life.

My husband would come home from his work trips while I was dealing with extreme psychological states and everything was such a mess. He would find dirty dishes with food stuck on them, loads of unwashed clothes lying about, and clutter scattered around the house. I felt guilty but just didn't have it in me to accomplish my responsibilities; my pain totally consumed me, and I had so little strength. It felt like it took every ounce of my strength to just stay alive. I was so tired of having to pretend I was okay during the times I ventured out in public.

Note: While writing this I realized how unjust it is that a rapist or child abuser can get as little as a few years in prison when the victim gets a life sentence. Being raped as a child has affected every single piece of my being at every single age and moment of my life. Hmm, something's really wrong there!

During this difficult time, I talked to my children about how I was going through something rough but that I was okay, and I was healing.

I assured them that none of it was their fault. I don't go for pretending things are okay with my family when they're not. Children always know, and it's important to explain that the problem isn't their fault and that their parent is going to be all right. Make sure you don't give your children more information than they can handle. Just say a few words to acknowledge something is going on. I find the whole mystery and elephant-in-the-room approach to be secretive, confusing, and scary for children. And it usually makes them angry when they do find out. They're part of the family and part of the support, and they learn how to deal with trauma from watching you.

PART III

Sexual Assault Intervention Services

Soon after I contacted my local sexual assault services, their sexual assault counselor (SAC), Patti, called me back. Soon, I met with Patti to start treatment, which began with psychoeducation about what posttraumatic stress disorder (PTSD) and flashbacks are. As I explained what I had been going through for eight months, she couldn't believe I hadn't been bedridden or hospitalized. I wanted to collapse in her lap. I was so grateful to God for bringing someone into my life who understood what I was going through and believed in my account of what was happening to me.

> *That led to my finally being diagnosed in 2007 with post-traumatic stress disorder—after living with the symptoms for a quarter-century. Most trauma victims do not develop full-blown PTSD, but* ***more than 80 percent of victims of childhood sexual abuse*** *will experience some symptoms of the disorder.*
>
> —Dawn Eden[16]

Patti told me that my state of residence had a program that would provide treatment *free* to anyone who had been raped at any point in his or her life. It didn't matter if it was thirty years ago or yesterday. The program was free, so there were no barriers to helping those

---

16 Dawn Eden, *My Peace I Give You* (Notre Dame: Ave Maria Press, 2012), 75.

victimized by rape. I can't even begin to tell you how enormously grateful I am to my state government for these services and especially my amazing SAC. That service was my lifeline, and I don't even want to think about how things might have gone for my family and me had I not had a caring and knowledgeable SAC to guide me. I was barely hanging on.

A huge way Patti helped me was by using psychoeducation to explain Complex-PTSD, flashbacks, and grounding techniques. Complex-PTSD, or C-PTSD, is a form of PTSD that comes from trauma over a prolonged time in childhood. Its core characteristics are psychological fragmentation or compartmentalized memories, feelings, and parts of self; loss of a coherent sense of self (e.g., I'm not sensing myself); loss of a sense of safety, trust, and self-worth; and a tendency to be re-victimized. It also manifests in difficulty regulating emotions, explosive rage, forgetting traumatic events (repression), and feeling detached from mental processes and the body. As I studied these aspects with Patti, I finally understood why I had such trouble controlling my body and cognitive functions after flashbacks. In addition, a person may struggle with numbness, persistent anxiety, and a hyper-aroused state that leads to problems with anger, addictions, and risky behaviors.

Most importantly, my SAC explained how the flashbacks are memories being relived. Sometimes these memories do not contain the visual aspect. They are raw memories being released into consciousness. She provided so many answers to the mysterious things I was experiencing and gave me grounding techniques to help me cope—stomping my feet on the floor, saying my current age, date, time, etc. These tools allowed me to stay grounded in the present moment instead of making me feel I was being attacked in the past.

Do those symptoms sound familiar? I had been journaling about these things for years, and yet Patti so perfectly described my torment when she barely knew me. How did she know all of that? You mean there's a name for it, and many others experience this hell too? There's treatment specifically for what I'm going through? I was elated to hear this, and it gave me so much comfort and hope. I wasn't insane. I was no longer alone with this pain!

Can you imagine suffering so much distress then going to see a counselor who describes in detail what you have been dealing with for a long time? I was relieved and so grateful.

Next, my SAC recommended the book *The Courage to Heal: A Guide for Women Survivors of Child Sexual Abuse* by Ellen Bass and Laura Davis, which I obtained right away. It turned out to be my healing-from-trauma bible, and it described things I thought no one else could know. I was shocked that other people experienced similar feelings and behaviors to those I'd been living with. It was such a powerful aid in helping me understand the stages of healing, and it allowed me to identify with other women's stories. Other people have not only lived through it but have come out on the other side. They were actually thriving!

Patti used Trauma-Focused Cognitive Behavioral Therapy or TF-CBT. This treatment approach entails working with trauma education, mood regulation, gradual exposure to triggers, and cognitive distortions—like victims' belief that the abuse was their fault and that they are damaged and worthless. The treatment addressed the C-PTSD pieces that deal with three fundamental areas: 1) emotional dysregulation, 2) pathological dissociation, and 3) stress-related breakdowns, such as with bodily health.

Emotional dysregulation refers to moods shifting uncontrollably. I could relate to that! The erratic emotions are similar to the inconsolable distress a young child will experience if unable to form a secure attachment to a primary caregiver. I could relate to that too!

Pathological dissociation is the robotic feeling of being in a daze or acting on autopilot. It's like being in a dream, being unable to control your body with a sensation of emotional and cognitive overload, and a general feeling of being overwhelmed. During the attacks when I was a child, I couldn't get away or fight them off, so I went into a state of immobility. It's similar to what happens in the animal kingdom when an organism perceives a threat and prepares for attack by surrendering in a numbed state.

The breakdown in bodily health comes from feeling hypervigilant or on constant high alert in a chronic state of stress, along with experiencing the flashbacks. I had a nervous system that was constantly on edge. I journaled an example of how my sense of feeling unsafe was a cause of the high-alert experience:

> *Scared and out of control, nowhere to hide, left out there to be hurt, unsafe. What is around the next corner? Who will hurt me next? The world is a terrifying place.*

My flashbacks continued for over another year with months in between episodes. Throughout those months, I would get the picture memories over time, usually during quiet times in a bath or while meditating.

One day after another flashback event, as I was coming to and journaled what I saw, I said out loud assertively and wrote the words, "I am in control and I let the grip of this event go. I let it go." That statement was something the ex-monk recommended. I liked how self-empowering that declaration felt. Lastly, I gave thanks for the mystery being solved and for the spiritual support I was receiving.

All told, I had a flashback with my hypnotherapist, one with my ex-monk alternative practitioner, one in my car, a few alone at home, a mini one with my SAC and my ADD nurse practitioner, and one with my husband. Finally, so many of my questions were answered, and I knew the truth. The truth I had been trying to reach for many years had been inside me the whole time.

* * *

One day while meditating, I closed my eyes and had a powerful vision of eight men. I think three of the men represented the neighborhood man (the repeat offender), three of them were the three teen boys, one from the attack when I was four, and the last one was from the barn rape.

Eight Beheaded Men

> *I can vaguely see eight men on their knees in the distance. I have a huge saber, and I take their heads off with one powerful swing. Then I drop the sword and feel awful as I fall to my knees. Revenge is not what I really want; I want release. Suddenly, I see a beautiful pure light and the outline of a person. I sense it is Jesus. He takes my hand, and I ask Him, "What is your will for me, Jesus?" He replies, "Have pity and compassion on them. Pray for pure light in their hearts."*

> *I can barely make out one of the men, who along with the other men, has his head back on now, and I speak compassionately to the man as I forgive him. It feels peaceful and good to do this, whereas chopping his head off did not. Jesus says, "You can let it go now. This one is done."*
>
> *I see there was a cord or energetic connection between the man and me. A Holy One hands me his saber, and I cut the cord. I understand this symbolizes cutting the attacker's hold on me. The rapist's end recoils into his body, and mine shrivels up into nothing.*

Each time throughout my journey, and especially during and after the crisis phase, a deep spiritual forgiveness brought profound healing and considerable awareness.

My AS could have compassion for the rapists because I knew they were spiritual beings at their core, and I believed they were sick, damaged people crying out for help. Maybe if they had been loved and treated with forgiveness and compassion when they were children, they wouldn't have been attacking others. It was so clear that revenge only fostered more hatred, which would lead to more attacks. However, I needed to go through more experiences with my child self reaping revenge before I was ready to wholly internalize forgiveness.

A few days after the Eight Beheaded Men vision, I was still processing the images, and I felt moved to write the following poem in my journal.

Held No More

I hold my head up high
High to the sky
I am lovely
I am loved
I am strong, beautiful, and clean
He (rapist) holds me down in hell no more
His dark strangling grip behind my mind
I pray for him and let him go
Freedom, Freedom
I can fly
Because
I'm held in hell no more

****

In my journey to forgive my abusers, I would experience progress, taking a few steps forward. Then I would step back. The steps forward would trigger a rebound effect when I got scared of the new feelings from the growth. I wasn't used to these new ways of relating, and I would regress a bit and then recover, moving even further forward from where I had left off.

* * *

By this point, I was forty-four years old. I had just had another flashback and was preparing to go on a work trip with my husband and children to Boston. I was not doing well, but fortunately, the really intense mood states would periodically lighten up. I journaled this at the beginning of the trip, while in rough shape alone in the hotel room:

I feel so broken—I'm shut down. The fear, the pain. Like there is an ocean of agony right in front of my face. I want out, so I shut down. I could sit and not move—stare into space indefinitely. So overwhelmed. My desire to drink is intense. I can't imagine there is enough alcohol to help me. A lost cause. I'm terrified I will have a flashback with my kids in a public place in the city. Please no. I don't feel safe. Too vulnerable to be away from home and my support network. Too scared to go to a new AA meeting with all strangers.

I was so full of emotion I had to express it. Consider the following poem and picture.

TRAPPED

I'm in a cage.
A prison of pain.
Trapped in an endless
Sea of agony.
I'm broken, cracked,
Damaged goods.
I want to hide
Numb from the torment and
The endless work
I feel trapped.

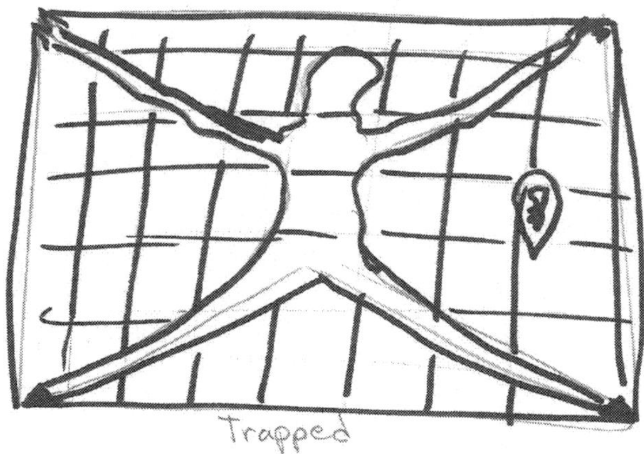
Trapped

****

At this point, I felt alone and in such distress while my husband and children were at the pool. I got on my knees and cried out to Jesus to help me. I didn't know what else to do; I was at the end of my rope and trying so hard to hold it together, to hold on to my sanity. Then, I walked into the lobby where there was a bar. I looked at it longingly. I thought, *There isn't enough alcohol to numb this pain, and if I still feel the urge to drink this strongly when I wake up, I will drink tomorrow.*

I went outside to have a smoke to distract myself, and a woman appeared out of nowhere. She asked me for a light, and we talked. When I told her I was originally from New Jersey, she said, "I'm from Boston, and I'm here to run the marathon. But I was born at Muhlenberg Hospital in New Jersey." First of all, I was shocked a marathon runner was smoking! It just seemed so out of place, and then I couldn't believe she was born at the same hospital I was. What are the chances of that?

We chatted for a while. Then I turned to put out my cigarette. When I looked back to her, she was gone. I believe she was an angel because there was something odd but beautifully comforting about my encounter with her that I couldn't explain. I felt peace. Can you believe it? This happened right after the intense level of pain I had just been in. My desire to drink was gone as I walked back into the hotel. That experience still blows my mind! Thank you, God, for your merciful grace.

Some people think that to be strong is to never feel pain.
In reality, the strongest people are the ones who feel it,
understand it, accept and learn from it.
—Unknown[17]

The next morning, I took a shock therapy (freezing cold) shower, and my mood shifted to a lighter, more positive place. Since I wasn't feeling tormented, my drinking urges temporarily ceased. I felt more present for my family, which made it possible for the kids and me to enjoy some time at the aquarium.

While at the aquarium, I was aware of feeling better than the previous night, yet still raw and vulnerable. My whole being felt like an open wound. It was a distinct sensation I carried throughout my crisis phase. I needed something to comfort me.

While we were browsing the gift shop, a stuffed sea turtle caught my eye. Turtles are my favorite animal, and "Turtle" was one of

17 "To Be Strong Is to Experience Pain," *Positive Outlooks* (blog), January 14, 2014, https://positiveoutlooksblog.com/2014/01/14/to-experience-pain/.

my father's nicknames for me. I walked around the shop hugging this turtle, and it felt so good. I felt small and childlike. Instead of admonishing myself that I was an adult and was being ridiculous hugging the turtle, I told myself it was okay to be comforted, and then I bought it. I carried that stuffed turtle everywhere for the rest of the trip, pretending I was holding it for my daughter. Allowing my CS, who was right on the surface, this token of comfort was healing, as she was feeling acknowledged and cared for. She felt seen.

After the Boston trip, I had a couple of weeks' worth of a healing break. Luckily, these healing breaks would appear periodically to help me to gain strength for the next round. I would feel quieter and sleep better. I would also feel up to exercising and cooking healthy food. I really soaked up and appreciated these breaks, but at the same time, I couldn't help wondering what I would be confronted with next.

After that healing break, one day I was in the kitchen with my children and felt something awful rising up in me. My twelve-year-old son was at the kitchen desk doing homework, and my six-year-old daughter was sitting on the floor coloring. My automatic response to what I was experiencing was to scan the house in my panicked mind for anything to numb me, but I couldn't think of anything. Whatever it was, it felt like it was going to kill me—no exaggeration! I knew this time I would have to let this evil come up; I would have to face it once and for all. *Enough already!* Shaking and holding on for dear life, I grabbed onto the countertop. As my most hidden self-hatred rolled over me, I knew to ask for help. I stood my ground and tried to weather the coming storm with a prayer to God.

I feel a huge scary sensation in my solar plexus. All my strength, anything I can get my hands on, just keep it down at all costs, keep it down. If I let it bubble up, it will strangle me just like the rapists. They loved to put their hands around my neck and think about squeezing the life out of me. Their ultimate power was to take my body and then my life.

If I let this thing come up, I will crack, crumble, and disintegrate—I will DIE! I will disappear and never ever come back. It will swallow me up in the void, the point of no return, annihilation. ANNHILATION!

I feel able to move my body now, and I make my way into my bedroom for some privacy. The scary sensation is a raw **self-hatred** rising up. I am facing my fear mind. Then I go into it. The self-hatred is accompanied by this self-talk:

"You don't deserve to live. You dirty rotten moth-eaten worthless piece of junk. Nobody loves you! They all say they do, but nobody loves you because you suck because you are a whore. DIE, BITCH, DIE!"

> *"Oh God, help me, help me, please help me. Take me from this hell that just won't end. It goes on and on. The never-ending torment of my being. Death is the only answer. It just won't end. Make it stop. Get it out of me. I want a do-over. GET ME OUT OF HERE!"*

Then I wrote this poem as I had a vision of God coming to my aid to support me:

Escape

How I long to rest in the valley
Quiet peaceful clouds wisp by
I let go—completely
Limp, almost death-like
God holds what I can no longer bear
He reassures me, and I rest forevermore

****

God, without exception, would comfort me and help me through my pain. Each time I was able to tolerate a rape memory or another piece of self-hatred rising up into consciousness, I knew I was a little bit freer. In the moment, it felt unbearable, but once it was out in the open, I knew it couldn't keep gnawing at me like the parasite it was.

This was another pivotal moment of learning that fear wouldn't kill me and its only power was my belief in it. I learned I could look fear in the eye with God by my side and the fear would disappear. My fear of my fear only has power if I believe it does. Now I know I have the power over my fear. My true self is powerful. My power is in my belief in loving forgiveness.

My spiritual connection held me up. I used the tools I learned from different people and the book I mentioned, *The Courage to Heal*. I tried numerous exercises suggested in the book. One I liked was honoring my ability to cope and survive by listing coping behaviors. Here are some things I listed:

- forgetting (repressing memories)
- lack of integration (putting feelings, memories, and parts of

myself away in compartments so I didn't have to hold onto it all at once)

- leaving my body and spacing out (dissociation)
- being controlling (false sense of security)
- distracting myself with chaos
- self-medicating

All these coping behaviors allowed me to go on with my life, yet they were destructive. Instead, when I was ready, I needed to know the truth and replace negative coping behaviors with supportive ones as part of my healing.

The day after I did the above coping skills list exercise, I saw my SAC, Patti. She reminded me to live, despite the pain, until I could gain perspective and accept how I turned the guilt and shame on myself. The dynamic of internalizing shame is common in sexual assault survivors, and it was what the abusers wanted; they preyed upon that sense of shame. How many of you have experienced being blamed for your abuse and how wounding that has been?

Emotions, even painful ones, are here to tell you something. They are messages to be tended to. Yet how can you tend to something you don't know is there? Emotions must be acknowledged and felt; or else they cannot be learned from, grown from, or processed.

—Marianne Williamson[18]

18 Williamson, *A Course in Weight Loss*, 159.

Note: Please take this in. *Survivors, it wasn't your fault. Let your shame go; you don't deserve it. You deserve love, forgiveness, and support.* I want to say this to you: "I'm sorry for your suffering and struggle, for all the things that were done to you, for all the ways you've been wounded. You are a beautiful light in this world. May you have peace and healing."

PART IV

Through the Continued Darkness of Rage

Well into my second year of remembering, I began having rape-themed nightmares every night. These involved me being watched, stalked, and raped. The vision below helped me cope with my ensuing rage. My nervous system felt like it was on the brink of a breakdown. Spiritual help with my inner child work continued with this healing vision:

The Bodhi Tree

In meditation I see Kwan Yin, Goddess of Mercy, sitting at the base of the bodhi tree. All her beautiful wild animals are lying about her on a grassy knoll. I climb up the hill and ask if I can lie down. She says yes. The fresh scent of spring grass is in the air. I see my CS run to a Holy One, and He picks her up and hugs her while He blesses her. She loves Him so. Through my adult eyes, I watch and cry while my heart fills with gratitude and hope for my lost little girl self.

Buddha sits at the base of the tree now. My CS is handed to Buddha while Kwan Yin pours a drop of love and compassion from her vase onto my little head. It flows over my CS's body as she becomes pure light: first her head, then her heart, then her whole being.

> *My AS hugs my CS now as she says, "I feel good. I'm happy." My AS says, "Little Marie, you will never be hurt again, and there is no need to be afraid anymore because the Holy Ones are always with you." My CS just keeps repeating, "I feel good." She jumps up and asks my AS to play, so we run through the woods pretending to be fairies. My CS is so full of life, and at this point my AS is wearing my baby self in a sling. My CS, AS, baby, preschool, adolescent, and teen selves play Ring around the Rosie, and then we all lie down and rest in a field of flowers. It is wonderful to see my CS so alive, happy, and free. I give thanks to the Holy Ones for their support and loving compassion, and I tell them how deeply I love them.*

A couple of weeks after this vision, I had the flashback from my preschool age, which I mentioned earlier. During the session with Patti, I was talking about reading of a little girl being abused, and suddenly I was distinctly aware of my four-year-old self in my mind; curled up in the fetal position. I started to clench my fists as hard as a rock and was shaking. I was disassociating as my four-year-old self came to the surface, as I went back in time in my mind. I was being molested and wanted to yell, but instead I was turning it inward. My teen self came and said "You have a voice. It's okay to yell." My young self screamed, "STOPPPPPP!"

Patti jumped up to let others know we were okay. My child self wanted to scream more, but she held back. She wanted to yell, "Stop hurting me. You're mean." She wondered why someone would want to hurt her like that. She cried and made noises, and then my body went limp. As I came out of the memory, I struggled to breathe, my forehead felt like a concrete block, and I was sick to my stomach. I was thankful I had the strength to release that event and so grateful to have a safe person like Patti with me while I endured it.

After going home and telling my husband what happened in therapy, I went to bed. In my mind, I kept seeing that man standing over me. I couldn't get rid of that frightening image of his erect penis right before my eyes! Later, my husband comforted me, and then I went to the bathroom and gagged. It felt like I needed to get something out of me. The next day I felt aches and pains from my head to my hips, and my jaw was sore from all the clenching. Throughout the days following this flashback, I felt young and incapable of fulfilling my adult responsibilities. I felt far away from my husband and children, and I wanted to stay in bed in the fetal position, but I didn't.

Patti talked to me about acceptance. So, I took her lead and acknowledged that I accepted myself. I was proud of the hard healing work I was doing. I was enough, and whatever I could get done was enough for now; whatever I could remember was enough to bring healing.

My SAC explained that when I dissociated, which was my mind's way of protecting itself, I was elsewhere, outside my body. The combination of not being able to connect normally to the experience, along with the trauma memories being stored differently, made it difficult to retrieve complete memories with all the details.

Patti also talked to me about how I wouldn't get all my questions answered about my attacks, but I could accept that what I did get was enough for my heart to heal.

We cannot change anything until we accept it.
Condemnation does not liberate, it oppresses.
—Carl Jung[19]

* * *

A huge piece of my crisis phase was my attempt to hold onto my life as a wife and stay-at-home mom, while accepting how limited and debilitated I was at times. Just the energy it took to try to look normal and function in the smallest ways felt too hard to do. I really tried to hide what I could from my family. Can you relate to this experience of being burdened with your trauma to the point of barely being able to function?

The flashbacks and extreme moods were exhausting and painful, and my hypervigilance of adults around children was also tiring. I would get a distinct feeling of disintegrating or coming apart at the seams, like that drawing with *The Gold* poem. My state of being scared me and made me wonder how long I could keep hanging on. I wrote in my journal:

> *Tired and down, beaten down. I just want to rest. I can barely handle the kids. I feel broken, weak, and vulnerable. Holding onto life, sanity, and any normalcy I can.*

I'll bet many of you can relate to the journal entry above; I'm sorry you can. Then I drew the following picture, *Holding On*, and I wrote the *Soul Ravage* poem. Afterward, I drew the *Rip It Out* picture. *Bam, bam, bam,* these came up one after the other.

---

19 "Carl Jung Quotes," BrainyQuote, accessed January 16, 2018, https://www.brainyquote.com/quotes/carl_jung_101266.

HOLDING ON

****

SOUL RAVAGE

Rage is pain
In the deep, dark crevices of my being
Fire, power, destruction
I'm disintegrating
It's too hard to keep up the fight to heal
Decompensation
Looking in my window from another floor
Are you ready yet?
Have you had enough?
Thrashing, ripping, tearing
Screaming, "Get it out!"
I want it out, get it out now
Crush it, pound it, sever it, and bury it.
My rage eats at the core of my soul.
It ravages my true self,
and swallows me alive.
My rage is my pain!

****

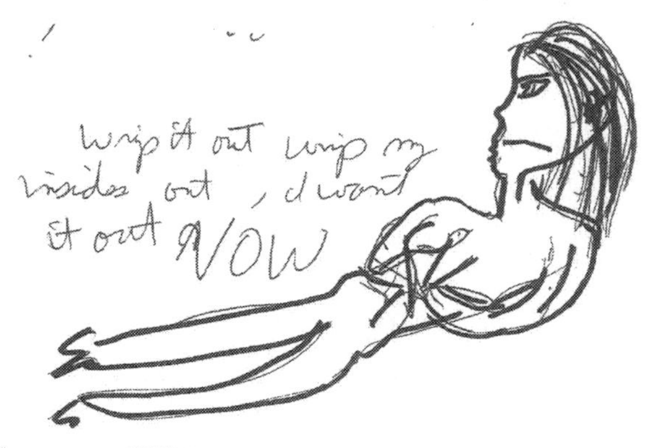

****

Rage, one of the many wonderful life-giving gifts sexual trauma survivors get to deal with. Yeah, right! Do you understand why all this pain was repressed? Can you imagine a child or teen trying to cope with this seemingly endless barrage of emotional agony? I think if I had remembered when I was younger, without the needed support to deal with it and heal, I wouldn't have been able to hold hope for an end to the pain; I would have just checked out of life.

After writing the above journal entries, I sat on the floor of my bedroom with a large drawing pad and drew a violent and disturbing picture of what I wanted to do to my mother for not protecting me. I wrote about what I was doing to her and the rapists. Once again, so much rage and blame went to Mother. I wanted to blame someone who was responsible for me and someone who felt safer to blame than me. My mother was a safe and easy target of my rage. What about my father? What about me?

Note: I eventually came to realize that most of my rage was actually directed at myself because I blamed myself for all my pain. This truth was so devastating that I had to keep it hidden, and that dark truth was that I falsely believed there was something wrong with me that caused my mother and the rapists to behave the way they did. **I realized it was me who I needed to forgive and love, and I needed to learn how to let go of the untruths I held about myself.** When I took those steps with God's help, my deepest wounds healed permanently.

I found I needed healthy, positive outlets for rage. Patti suggested getting some cheap dishes and breaking them on a blanket in the garage as one example. I found that writing and drawing helped, and I tried yelling when I was home alone or in my car; these strategies were what worked for me. My SAC reminded me that I didn't need to be afraid of rage or hold it in. Instead, I needed to release it to find healing. The wise healer within me knew what I needed to do. I needed to trust and listen to myself.

> *What is not love is fear. Anger is one of fear's most potent faces. And it does exactly what the fearful ego wants it to do: It keeps us from receiving love at exactly the moment when we need it most.*
>
> —Marianne Williamson[20]

At my low times, my husband and friends helped me by listening, offering to drive me to an AA meeting, watching my kids for a while, offering to pay someone to clean my house, or having a cup of tea

20 Marianne Williamson, *Illuminata: A Return to Prayer* (London, UK: Penguin Books, 1994), 134.

with me. Each act of kindness strengthened me. It was surprising how even the smallest gesture was deeply comforting. I'm very grateful. It felt right to not be the strong one or the one doing a lot of helping.

It felt good to be able to receive support, accept that I needed it, and honor where I was at. This would sometimes be accompanied by a healing break and the ability to acknowledge my progress. I wrote the following entry in my journal at one of these positive points:

> *I feel grounded and strong today. I feel good. My greatest gift is my spiritual connection. I can't get that on the physical plane. I'm growing, and my heart is healing. I'm getting stronger and stronger. Gratitude.*

* * *

Around this time, my mother and her boyfriend were planning to celebrate their thirtieth anniversary together at the seashore, and they invited me and my family. My mother's relationship with her boyfriend was very unstable and complicated, and it caused a lot of pain for me. I was also in the throes of the crisis phase, feeling raw and vulnerable. I immediately took all the work on myself. How was I going to keep myself safe enough to endure this weekend? The operative words being *safe* and *endure*! I was scared I could have a flashback at any moment. I was planning on therapy, lots of AA meetings, etc. What was I thinking? I could just refuse to go, right? Well, that isn't how it played out.

My AA sponsor said if it were her, she wouldn't go on the anniversary weekend because it was a big setup for trauma triggers and a drinking relapse. It was clear to those close to me that it was not a good idea either, but it took me a little while to see that.

At one point, my teen self finally set me straight. One day I closed my eyes to rest and immediately saw my teen self, and she was pissed off at me!

> *"I'm so mad! You make me go to the beach weekend with them and I will make you drink, you bitch. Leave me alone! Stop bringing this shit up. I don't want to go there. The hell with their thirty years together, and she wants me to celebrate it—GO TO HELL! I don't want to go, and you will be sorry if I do. All bets are off. It's revenge time."*

Damn! That was as clear as it gets. Not a good idea to go. I finally got the message. Then my AS talked to my teen self:

> *"I want to hear your truth. You had to tolerate and put up with so much. Mom really messed up. We had to watch him be abusive with her too. It was so hard.* **I promise you, Teen Marie, I won't make you withstand him on the anniversary weekend. We will stay home.** *I'll work it out and cancel. I love you, and I want to honor you and respect your wishes. Yes, you have the right to say no. It's done.*
>
> *"We are in this life together, we are partners. You don't have to do everything and figure out everything on your own anymore. You have me, Adult Marie, to hear you, protect you, comfort you, validate you, and act on your behalf. We don't have to drink over this. You have a healthy adult who loves you and takes care of you. I will tell Mom, 'No, thank you, it's not a good time for us to go, and it's not up for discussion.'"*

I discussed all this with my SAC, who helped me come up with statements to tell my mother that my family would not be attending her anniversary weekend. I called my mother and told her what I needed, and she respected my wishes not to discuss it, which I appreciated. My counselor pointed out the importance of my teen and adult selves being allies. I also had several revelations during this experience. I realized I didn't have to work hard and endure the weekend. I could instead choose to take care of myself and my family *first.* I realized I didn't have to feel bad about hurting my mom's feelings. She made her choices, and there were consequences that go with them. I was allowed to make my own choices too. It was not my problem. I could take care of me and have peace with that. The opportunity to say no to going on the weekend trip ended up being a lesson in empowerment and building strong boundaries.

Spiritual mastery involves building the mental, emotional, and behavioral habits to carry you through such times without an explosion of dysfunctional behavior.
—Marianne Williamson[21]

21 Williamson, *A Course in Weight Loss*, 172.

PART V

The Warrior Emerges

One day well into the crisis phase, I was driving to Jack's (the ex-monk's) office for a treatment with my children. Everything started to feel far away, and I got worried. I questioned what was happening. Was it a flashback coming on? I arrived in the parking lot with my children—thirteen and seven years old—and knew I was in trouble. My whole body was shaking, and everything looked blurry. I called from my car and asked Jack and Ellen to come out and help me in. As Jack's wife, Ellen, walked me back to a room, I walked into a wall. I wasn't fully present.

Finally, I made it into the treatment room away from my children and others. I thought, *Please don't let my kids see me having a flashback.* I knew one was on the way, as I felt myself uneasily going back in time to when I was young. I suddenly watched myself go down to the floor, struggling and making sounds. Men came in from the waiting room to hold me down, so I wouldn't hurt anyone or break anything. While on the hard floor, I saw the adjustment table next to me. I must have been coming back to the present moment. Everyone came into view and looked upset. I felt so incapable of being an adult. I felt broken once again.

That flashback was interrupted because of the men holding me down. It wasn't good, but I understand why they needed to restrain me. As a result, it was very short. Seconds? Minutes? I'm not sure. My husband was called to come get me since I was a mess and unable to drive. I shuffled along to the car, mumbling and repeating things like, "No no no no no" under my breath. My children saw me that way too. I wish they hadn't.

When I got home, I sat on the floor of my bedroom by myself and drew words on large pieces of paper, many of them. I felt very young and wrote things in big awkward black letters like:

"NO DON'T HURT ME—I HIDE"

"I CAN'T COME OUT—SCARED—MA MA MA MA MA MA MA MA MA MA"

"HIDE ME, GO AWAY—NOOO"

"PAIN PA PA PA PA PA PA PA PA PAIN"

"HIDE HI HI HI"

"I SMALL I GO NOW BYE BYE NO NO NO NO"

I drew one scribble picture with green, red, and mostly black all over the page, like a traumatized preschooler might draw. I figured out it was my preschool-age self who had regressed to an even younger stage after being raped at four. My four-year-old self got to really express how awful she felt for the first time. God bless her heart.

It devastates me to take in my pain during those years. How I wish I could go back in time to reach a lifesaving hand out to my child self and save little me. But I think I did do that, it was just years later. I'm grateful I got the opportunity to hold my younger selves while they finally experienced being heard, protected, loved, and cherished. I was their loving witness. And I'm also glad I got to thank them for surviving it all. As we kept working on healing together (my CS and AS), a warrior emerged in me.

Soon after the above flashback, I was soaking in a healing bath and had a powerful vision. It helped me see that I was progressing and getting stronger, which had a great impact on me.

I, the Warrior

I am on a beach, and a muscular dark-skinned man approaches. I look into his eyes only to see evil intent. He picks me up and carries me across the rugged terrain. When I reach out to touch him, his face turns into a dragon head with a huge mouth and teeth. He swiftly takes a bite out of my upper abdominal area and leaves a gaping hole.

I don't even flinch. I Will NOT BE A VICTIM THIS TIME! I jump down out of his arms and hit his breathing acupuncture point with a dragon fist. The position of my hand takes his breath away. With great speed, I move my right hand down to his left hand and forcibly back up, karate chopping the left side of his neck and then striking his neck with my right elbow. Then I karate chop the right side of his neck.

The man doesn't know what hit him. He's completely caught off guard by my courage and ability to protect myself. I twist his head and break his neck. As he falls, I knee him in the groin. Next, I go behind him and reach around to gouge his eyes out. This prick won't be able to see or rape anyone ever again. This time I am the trickster, the surprise attacker, and this time I will be able to protect myself from the scariest of creatures.

We are at the edge of a cliff now, and I kick the man off into the ocean. He has the head and tail of a dragon and the body of a man. I climb down the cliff and slowly drag his limp body up the entire rock face to the highest point with incredible strength. This is when I put my right foot on him, raising my right arm up to the heavens with a sword outstretched. I yell out powerfully with guttural sounds of victory, "NO LONGER AM I A VICTIM!"

I feel courageous. I feel like Kali, with no fear of any kind, just total confidence and power. I watch as days pass and the vultures devour his carcass, just as I have devoured his life. I wear his bones as a necklace and as a symbol of the warrior I've become.

****

WOW! That vision was an awesome expression of my progressing from feeling like a small victimized child to a powerful warrior! The dragon piece was telling, since I was born in the year of the dragon and dragons are a sign of overcoming something hugely negative in one's life. This was a marker of my progress.

The female mother/warrior I had seen during my shadow self work a few years earlier was identified by my first therapist as Kali, a Hindu goddess who was a protective mother and destroyer of evil. After this vision, I was surprised to see pictures of Kali online; in them, she had one of her right hands holding a sword upright and her right foot on a male corpse with bones or sculls around her neck. How wild are those similarities to my vision?

I still had progress to make, such as moving from rage and revenge to forgiveness and peace. But for now, I was shifting from a scared child to a warrior, and I knew it. How grateful I felt not to be at the mercy of the evildoers in this world. When I felt small, I felt wide open to attack. Now, I felt mature; I could call on my warrior self whenever I needed her.

In that vision, the dragon man took a piece of me and left a gaping hole, just like the rapists did. I had felt so empty for so long. Can you identify with that experience of emptiness? I know about that wound, that well of damage, and I now know that it was healing. I was experiencing how to fill that gaping hole of emptiness with the empowering energy of healing self-love.

After this vision, I told Patti that I felt like a walking miracle, being able to survive the pain, torment, and dysfunction I had lived through. My relentless fight to heal and ability to function as well as I had all my life was a testament to strength. In the same way, your fight to live and heal is a testament to your strength. All that time I was holding my trauma secrets as they slowly killed me off. But now, the secrets were exposed, and I was alive and on my way to thriving. It took a long time for me to acknowledge my strengths, and I'm grateful to Patti for being instrumental in that process. Acknowledging my strengths was an important self-empowerment tool for recovery.

* * *

I was on my prayer mat one day when I had a memory. I saw the visual part of the rape from when I was 10–13 years old at the man's home near the woods that I described earlier. Then I processed it:

> *From where I sit on the prayer mat, I ask for the energetic cord between the rapist and me to be cut, and it is. I say aloud, "I am in*

control, and I let the grip of this event go. I let it go now." Then I talk to my ADS about how sorry I am that she was brutally raped. She didn't deserve any of it. The rapist was a sick man taking out his torment on her and saying mean things to her to make himself feel okay about hurting her. He was justifying his criminally insane acts by blaming her, and HE WAS WRONG!

We cry, cough, gag, growl, and shake together as we release the event. My ADS says, "He hurt me so bad over and over again. Why? I'm a nice person. Why do I get hurt? He stole, he robbed me." My AS continues to comfort her, and then my other age parts (baby, toddler, etc.) appear, and we rest around a circular pond of still waters with Jesus in His Grace.

*I keep repeating, "***Secrets kill, no more secrets, we are free, secrets kill, no more secrets, we are free***." At some point, I visualize my CS stabbing that rapist in his basement. At the end of the ICW vision, I ask to see a clear picture of his face, but it's blurry, which is disappointing. I still thank the Holy Ones for their help because I know I couldn't have remembered any of it without them and their support.*

I was a mess after this memory, and I dissociated to cope with it. It took some time to come back to myself, and I had many feelings to process in the memory's wake. A couple of days later, while on the way to an AA meeting, I was overcome by rage. I saw myself murdering that rapist over and over.

I break his neck, gouge out his eyes, rip out his heart, and pull off his penis. I scream over and over like I have never screamed before. My screams feel like they're coming from my toes. After the meeting, I still have so much rage. How could this happen to me? I feel so vulnerable and on the edge of insanity. The world and everything in it feels threatening. I am scared, hiding, and looking at everyone and everything with suspicion. Will that one hurt me too? I'm afraid that if I encounter a pedophile I'll attack him. I want to scream. I want to hide in bed. Everyone leave me alone! I'm not safe to be around. I might lose it and scare you.

Three days after the prayer mat memory, I had the associated flashback from that rape. That night, I recorded in my journal.

(**SHIELDS UP**) *My son was with me playing by my bed. I felt raw and shaky. I asked him to give me some time alone and started to really shake, cry, and pant, as I fell to the floor. I got up in a daze and stumbled my way to my husband in the den on the other side of our home. He saw me shuffling and looking tormented and got up to hug me. I shook like crazy and slipped through his arms like water spilling onto the floor. Suddenly, I was moving very fast, struggling, choking, and coughing. The feeling in the air was so intense—palpable terror!*

I was experiencing that cellar rape as if it were happening right then. I was barely aware of my surroundings, and I felt young. My husband went to close the door so our children wouldn't hear me while I was flailing about on my stomach. All I saw was a door shutting, and a jolt of terror ran through my spine as a premonition of impending death. I rushed to stop the door closing and thought, If he closes the door, he will surely kill me. I let out a bloodcurdling scream that rocked my home.

My husband was trying to contain me and kept telling me I was safe and at home with him. He comforted me and helped me come back to myself and get grounded. I was so confused and scared with the pain and shame and rage all at once. It was just an enormous torrent of fight-or-flight energy until I went limp. Unfortunately, my son heard me and was upset and had trouble sleeping. I couldn't sleep either. (**DEEP BREATH**)

I felt that flashback coming on for a couple of days. It's difficult to describe what the pre-flashback experience is like. I can feel something coming, but I don't know what it is or when it will manifest. After the flashback, I felt small, had trouble with my speech, and was very disoriented. I would jump at the smallest noise and experienced so many symptoms disrupting my ability to function while I slowly came back into my body.

Note: Trauma memories are challenging because they aren't stored as normal memories, and parts of them are clearly remembered while other parts are difficult to decipher and may be hazy. Also, parts of them are missing or fragmented. For example, with the memories above, I can remember the feeling parts, what was being done to my body, what was said to me, and what my body was doing in response. On the other hand, details like the time of day, the specifics of the person attacking me, and what location where I was being attacked, were all unclear.

* * *

Allow yourself to grieve. You will learn in time to be with the void, addressing it with a bubble bath rather than a sandwich, and with prayer time rather than a candy bar. Your task is to inhabit the emptiness, breathe through it, learn its lessons, and hear the message it conveys.

—Marianne Williamson[22]

22 Williamson, *A Course in Weight Loss*, 173.

Thankfully, healing experiences began to show up more frequently, and they helped me continue. One day while my kids were at school, I was in my bed again floating in and out of sleep and prayer. I knew once I picked up my children, it would be nonstop with snacks, homework, trying to act normal, making dinner, and doing the bedtime routine. So while I had an opportunity to rest and pray, I drifted into a vision and then journaled about it.

I say the Rosary and contemplate Jesus's suffering. I offer my suffering to Him and ask to be healed so I can better serve Him, my family, and the wounded like me. My heart feels full after the prayer. While I meditate, Jesus calls all my different age parts to Him and wraps us up together as one person. He touches the part of my spine that holds trauma energy with his staff, and it looks healed. He touches my third eye, and I see a bright light.

My different age parts feel peace and joy, and we play in a field full of flowers and then sit down to rest by calm waters with Jesus. There is a pillar of light in the center of the pond, and the light from each of our third eyes connects to each other and then to the pillar of light reaching to the heavens and to each of our hearts. Then we become one.

Gratitude

My cup overfloweth
Gratefulness at my core
For my Lord Jesus Christ
He holds me and heals me
I fall into His grasp
And my heart fills with His Holy love
I am healed
And I am free

The above vision was another validation of spiritual support and healing. More specifically, the different age parts of myself were integrating into one, my AS. I had taken another step along my healing journey.

I had a lot of guilt over all the time I spent on myself resting, journaling, and attending therapy and AA meetings. Instead, I should have been grateful for the difficult life-altering work I was accomplishing while still managing to hang onto life and support my family to whatever degree I could. I'm purposely including messages like this because I believe we survivors need to hear them.

I wanted my husband to know that when I was in bed, there was a good reason for it. The exhaustion and desire to rest were consuming. I would push myself each day to go on and at least get the minimum done, because it just wasn't in me to do more. When I felt okay, I wanted to do more and thrived on doing more, but I just couldn't when I was struggling. In reality, I was doing so much, but it was internally, within me. The inner work was huge, and thankfully, I kept up with my self-care enough that it shielded me from a physical breakdown.

In the fall of my forty-fourth year, I wrote a poem that inspired me. I hope it will inspire you too.

Wings of Grace

From Darkness into Light
From Torment into Peace
From coming apart at the Seams to
Streams of Whole Flowing Light
I ride the River of Pain and Release to Peace
To Freedom from Fright
To the Pure Light
The Dark Horse under the Blanket of the Void
Stands at my side
The Dark One waits while
The Pure Light Calls to me—"Come home"
Rest in the Hand of Love and be set free
To fly on the Wings of Grace where I belong.

****

I love that poem. It just warms my heart and gives me hope. It feels good to see more positive poems referencing release and healing.

My SAC said it was good that I went through a full range of emotions with each memory instead of getting stuck, and that I had effective ways of soothing myself. Learning how to soothe yourself is a big deal in the healing department. Have you thought about how you self-soothe or how you could self-soothe?

At this point, I had a long healing break of several months, so I took some time away from seeing my SAC. She reminded me that she was only a phone call away.

PART VI

The Unveiling of My Shame

My fellow survivors of childhood abuse, do you have a visceral knowledge of guilt and shame? This next journal entry about my ADS epitomizes how mine played out in such a ruthless way. I don't want to describe the rape in the gully behind my house by the neighborhood repeat offender, even though this one is not in the trauma chapter. Instead, I want to share other aspects related to it.

Over several days, I was periodically getting quick flashes in my mind while I was driving or showering or cooking. It was there, and then it was gone, only to return later. The same scene over and over. The flashes were of a girl around twelve to thirteen years old trying to climb up a hill on her hands and feet. The sense I got was that she was frantically scurrying up that hill, trying to escape. The hill looked like the gully behind the house I grew up in where I would go to smoke.

After many times of observing the same scene flashing by, I realized a flashback was approaching, and I felt tremendous dread. It finally came one day while I was home alone. I felt anxious, like my skin was crawling. I wanted to escape myself. I gave up trying to accomplish any household chores and sat quietly, allowing this monstrous feeling to come up. This is what I journaled.

I kept seeing a quick movie in my mind of my ADS frantically clawing at dirt, trying to escape up a hill. She didn't get far as I watched him drag her back down. Watching this made me feel unstable and shaky, like I wanted to curl up in a ball. I visualized my AS trying to comfort my ADS by telling her she was not alone and that we would walk through the pain together.

The flashback came along with memory fragments, and when the rape part stopped, I stumbled up the hill to my house. I wanted to RIP MY SKIN OFF! I remembered the shame and humiliation I felt. I thought, Just kill me now and get it over with. I can't take any more of this. No more rapes!

Then I turned on myself.

I didn't even get up the hill and I already started thinking, He's right, you are a piece of shit. You don't deserve to live. You were raped because you're evil. You disgust me. I hope you die, bitch. You asked for it. IT IS YOUR FAULT! The guilt, shame, and self-hatred were unbearable to hold in my consciousness, so those feelings also went where I couldn't find them—deep in my mind.

I made my way back to my house and went to my room, where I sat in my rocking chair feeling robotic and numb, holding my stuffed animals and spacing out, detesting myself with such passion and loathing life. Repeating "not again, I must be worthless, not again, it (rape) couldn't have happened again."

*Then my ADS curled up on my bed, my great escape, and I saw my AS and angels surround her as I moved from the memory into a healing vision. My ADS said, "Go the f*** away!" swinging punches at us. "F*** all of you. You are useless to me. No one helps me." What she didn't say was that she felt she wasn't worth being helped.*

Maybe that was partly why I didn't tell anyone about these attacks. I was scared by the rapists' threats, and deep down inside I didn't feel I was worth helping. My ADS grabbed a large knife and stabbed her heart. She lay there with hollow, lifeless eyes. She just couldn't take it anymore. She felt her body had betrayed her, adults had betrayed her, society had betrayed her, and that bastard kept coming back to kill her off some more. What would have happened if I told back then? How I wish I had been able to remember and tell someone.

*My ADS then continued with her rage toward my AS, who was a safe target: "I don't want to hear your flowery bullshit. You can't grasp the hell I'm in. I don't want your hugs and sympathy. You can go to hell for all I care. F*** you, and leave me alone! Take your inner child work and shove it up your ass." My AS just sat and listened with love. No judgment and no comment. I wanted to let my ADS express whatever she could. I totally got why she said what she said, and I knew love would follow behind it, but the rage had to come out. We had to first walk through hell and our fear before we could open to love.*

Then my AS told her, "It was not your fault. You didn't do anything wrong. You were a beautiful and wonderful child then, and you are a beautiful and wonderful person now. I love you and cherish you. I am very thankful for your courage to go on. You are so strong, and I wouldn't be here with my loving husband and children if you weren't able to survive. Because of your strength, you have made it possible for all our parts to heal and become one and for my AS to be here today. Thank you for surviving, my dear younger self."

Note: Please take this in and think of saying those words to yourself, because some or all of these sentiments are your truth also. Look at yourself in the mirror. Use the words above, or your own, and speak them over and over as you look lovingly into your beautiful eyes. May God bless you with Divine Grace.

It was devastatingly painful to tap into my ADS, and scary too, but I knew I needed to do it. There was so much pain on my adolescent's face in that vision. That anguished face I used to draw before I remembered my trauma—I recognized it again in this memory.

Note: You may be thinking, *Why doesn't she tell someone?* The reasons are complicated from personal experience; survivors know this to be true. The combination of repressing the memories (not being able to remember), feeling like I was bad and at fault, and fearing the rapists' threats kept me silent. Each rape that occurred made it even harder to cope with all the complex aspects of telling, especially not being able to remember.

The hatred my ADS expressed was directly related to the fact that she blamed herself for the attack. This is a common reaction of victims; the self-blame results in shame and rage. Being an impressionable young girl and hearing the appalling things the rapists spewed at me made me question myself and even believe the lies. Several of the rapists said dreadful things. When I remembered as an adult, I was struck by how the rapists seemed to use a similar tactic of verbally degrading me. It was like it made what they were doing okay or somehow justified their behavior. They made themselves believe I wanted it or deserved to be attacked. On some level, they knew how awful their actions were and needed to convince themselves that it wasn't their fault.

Unfortunately, their lies fed my self-loathing and shame. The rapists' other purpose of degrading was to control and confuse. Nothing made sense. Boundaries were ignored, and everything I was taught about how people were supposed to act was wrong. As a young person, I found this to be so confusing! I already had a taste of how violent and sick these men were, and I believed they would follow through with their threats.

In turn, self-hatred and shame usually lead to emotional instability and endless acting out, which further leads to actions that are perplexing to both the survivor and those around him or her. Such high-risk behaviors can even be life-threatening and include addictions, eating disorders, prostitution, cutting oneself, and suicide. All of this gets played out daily in our sexuality, our ability to have healthy relationships, carrying extra weight or armor, starving ourselves to disappear, and even in dressing—being oversexualized or covering up with oversized clothes to hide our bodies. Basically, every aspect of our life is affected.

In her book *My Peace I Give You*, Dawn Eden expresses her own take on her risky behavior of cutting: "My desire to cut myself stemmed from the desire to get my mind off my mental pain. I felt that because I felt such violence in my soul, the right thing to do was to bring it out into my body."[23]

It's easy to see how living with unconscious hateful feelings made

23 Eden, *My Peace I Give You*, 71.

me feel I was bad, and how the shame and guilt I'd buried caused me to unconsciously want to punish myself. Finally, I understood why I would engage in self-destructive behaviors. I had to escape the pain and shame. No one took responsibility for the heinous rapes I endured, so I did. No one was punished, so I needed to be. Someone needed to take responsibility, damn it!

Throughout this time, I would remind myself who really was to blame and what choices they had made, explaining how *my rapes were not my choice but that survival was*. I did what I needed to do to live through the actual rape, and I survived. I reminded my younger selves, more than once, that they were not at fault, because it was something I needed to hear over and over. I needed a lot of reassurance to help deal with my distorted view of being at fault.

Another big mystery related to my self-blame was why the rapes kept happening. Was it me? Pattie Mallette, Justin Bieber's mom, expressed this same confusion regarding her own experience as a child. I identified with her questions because I felt perplexed by how I could be raped repeatedly.

> *What's wrong with me? What am I doing to attract sexual attention? Why am I such a magnet for abuse? Sex followed me, lurking in the dark corners waiting for the perfect ambush.*
>
> —Pattie Mallette[24]

When I did get in touch with my four-year-old self through ICW in my forties, my CS believed, *If only I were truly lovable, Mommy would protect me. She would be more careful about where I go and who I'm with.*

---

24 Pattie Mallette with A. J. Gregory, *Nowhere But Up: The Story of Justin Bieber's Mom* (Grand Rapids: Revell, 2012), 24, 26.

Mommy would pay more attention. It's too painful for small children to be angry with their primary protector, so they bury it and then turn it on themselves. Children's egocentricity makes them believe everything that happens is about them, so it must be their fault when something bad happens. As a result, my guilt and shame process grew like a disease replicating cells, secretly infecting my whole self.

I learned that people who want to hurt children have what seems like a radar for finding those that feel damaged and vulnerable. They sniff out the neglected children that crave attention and approval, those who are so damaged that they don't recognize danger normally. By the time danger is detected, it's too late—they're already being attacked, degraded, and traumatized again. As the layers of trauma increase, so does the victim's vulnerability, adding more fuel for self-loathing and blame, all of which is internalized. Can you see the cycle here? Each trauma makes the next one more probable. It's perplexing. Instead of making a survivor more aware and able to avoid the trauma, the damage makes the survivor less able to detect danger. There are so many layers of trauma. This is why so many rape survivors have multiple rapes in their lives!

> **Note:** My sexual assault counselor told me about the malfunctioning "yuk-o-meter" of a sexual trauma survivor. Basically, it's when someone doesn't sense danger normally. The person usually has damage due to trauma, and their internal warning system is broken because their boundary system has been broken.

Did you know the most common age for a child to be raped is nine or ten years old? I was nine or ten when the neighborhood sicko came into my house. I had enough inner demons dealing with the first rape at four years old. My mind was full of confusion. Later in my healing work as an adult working with my younger selves, I realized I felt marked, like damaged goods. "No one would really love me if they knew what had been done to me. I'm nothing now."

Such utter lies those beliefs were. Since my beliefs were secrets that were totally hidden from my conscious mind, I couldn't do anything about them, so they slowly killed parts of me off from deep within. I'm grateful I finally uncovered those secret misbeliefs, so I could address them as lies and tell myself the truth.

> *Many of us have shame, guilt, pain, and anger attached to things we have done or experienced. We go to great lengths to hide what we have done or what has been done to us. You are as sick as your* **secrets.** *Until you reveal, examine, and unpack the negative emotions attached to the secrets, thoughts, feelings, and experiences, you are held captive by them.*
>
> —Iyanla Vanzant[25]

* * *

Do you catch yourself doing things that just seem odd or are confusing to you? Do you find yourself in strange places in your home when you feel unsettled and vulnerable—such as lying on the floor in the fetal position or hiding in a closet or a tub? After remembering what I had been through, I also began to remember and understand odd or

---

25 Iyanla Vanzant, "Many of us have shame, guilt, pain, and anger attached to things we have done or experienced. We go to great lengths to hide what we have done or what has been done to us," Facebook, November 3, 2013, https://www.facebook.com/DrIyanlaVanzant/photos/a.163309680368572.34873.150253431674197/660806407285561/?type=3&theater.

idiosyncratic behaviors, illnesses, and coping skills I had experienced and developed while growing up. These behaviors are some examples of the far-reaching effects of abuse. Once again, it was helpful to be able to put the pieces of my complex puzzle of life together and say, "Oh, now I get it." As you read some of the symptoms below, you may find aspects of them that ring true for you too:

- Many survivors of childhood trauma experience learning issues, ADD, exhaustion, and a host of other physical symptoms, because the traumatized brain sends energy normally needed to form the brain, to survival areas instead. I had learning difficulties and ADD (not diagnosed until adulthood) and my learning issues were so pronounced that I was watching Sesame Street in the fourth grade (9–10 years old) with severely developmentally disabled kids. Fourth grade was the year the neighborhood rapist came into my house. I believe I was "checking out" or dissociating at school as a trauma response. The learning issues turned out to be dyslexia and auditory processing problems.
- Also, in the fourth grade, I suddenly couldn't walk. My mother took me to the doctor and had some medical tests done. After a week or so, all of the tests came back with nothing, and my doctor talked to me. He said, "Marie, there is nothing wrong with you, and I want you to walk out of here right now." He never asked me what was going on in my life. Well, I did walk out, and I was completely confused once again. As an adult, I realized that, in psychological terms, I was unconsciously using the conversion defense mechanism. That's when anxiety and emotional conflict can get expressed physically as paralysis or pain. It's a more primitive defense commonly used by children. It's shocking, but the fourth grade was also when my smoking

and drinking began. I was numbing and self-medicating with substances.

- There were these seemingly random but short-lived episodes of severe gastric attacks (pain, vomiting, and diarrhea) that I couldn't associate with any illness or food I had eaten. These gastric episodes scared me because they were violently intense. It was as if my body was trying to release something it just couldn't hold in any longer. In hindsight, I remembered how I would go into a panic with these gastric attacks, practically be standing on my head in pain. They would mysteriously appear and disappear within a day. My emotional state at these times mimicked my emotional states during my rapes and flashbacks. Interesting. I also had periodic episodes where I broke out in hives from head to toe; no one could ever identify a cause. I think they even coincided with my attacks.
- I was the only one in my family with asthma. Traumatized children tend to have asthma, which expresses their emotional distress through their bodies. From the perspective of alternative medicine, the lungs are associated with emotion.
- Incessant teeth grinding. Loud, odd sounds woke me up regularly at night. The teeth grinding and clenching were signs of anxiety.
- My first therapist, Georgette, without knowing any of my abuse background, determined that I skipped a phase of development called the latency phase. Freud's latent period of psychosexual development occurs during the grammar school years. At this time, sexual energy is quietly directed to socialization and hobbies, and one's sexual self is not active (i.e., latent).

In my case, after being raped at four, I didn't experience a normal latency phase. I was drawn to sexual pictures, looking at people's private areas in a curious way and exploring my body.

- When I tried sailing in races at my summer home, I would feel so alone and scared out on the lake by myself in my little Sunfish. I believe the fear triggered my repressed trauma. I would become paralyzed by fear or go into a trauma freeze state and sit motionless on the boat while it floated to the shoreline. At the time, I was totally bewildered by my behavior. I'm sure I looked terrified, and I know I felt ashamed just sitting on the boat unable to move, feeling so confused and helpless about it. Upon remembering the sailing experiences a few years into therapy, my mother confirmed what I remembered.
- I compensated for my deep feelings of being a bad seed by striving for perfection and people pleasing.
- I self-medicated with food and alcohol. By thirteen years old (seventh grade), I added drugs to my self-medicating mix but phased them out in college. I was on a daily mission to escape my feelings; at the same time, I knew I needed to look normal, do well in school, and stay out of trouble. I worked hard to keep my numbing behaviors under the radar and had my own layers of denial, so no one would try to address it, including me.

By the time I was sixteen, I couldn't function at all without numbing myself in some way.

—Pattie Mallette[26]

26 Mallette with Gregory, *Nowhere But Up*, 48.

- I went mute when I was around most teen males in high school that were slightly older. It was because of the teen boys' gang rape when I was in middle school. I consciously wanted to be my outgoing self, but unconsciously I wanted to disappear. My misbelief was that if I wasn't noticed, they wouldn't get any ideas and hurt me like the other teen boys had. My muteness was an expression of social anxiety from my previous traumas.
- An oddity about my older teens was that I didn't even own a pair of jeans, and I rarely wore pants for years in my twenties. How many teenagers and people in their twenties do you know that don't own a pair of jeans or like to wear pants?
- In college, I dressed like I was going to work on Wall Street every single day. Dressing in heels, stockings, and suits, I was all covered up. I'm sure I looked strange to the other students, but I was in denial of that. I was unconsciously trying to cover my private areas with A-line skirts and dresses in the hope that no one would look at me and get any ideas. On a deep level, I wanted to look unapproachable to male peers.

Those were some of my odd behaviors and illnesses, and I could have filled several pages with more, but now I understand why they happened. It's so interesting how it all made sense once I knew the truth and remembered my traumatic experiences. I see how my rapes perfectly line up with numbing coping behaviors like alcohol and paralysis. I finally got my answers.

PART VII

Holding On

Yes, I was holding onto hope for extended periods of relief, but I had some questions that kept coming up and causing anxiety.

- *Am I ever going to be well enough to go back to work?*
- *I'm afraid to build up my expectations of being a dependable, consistent worker when I feel so broken.*
- *I can sometimes function well from one hour to the next or one day to the next, but then suddenly be debilitated with depression and exhaustion. I wonder what my prognosis is?*
- *Will I always be haunted by my past with moods sneaking up behind me and shrouding me from the present?*
- *It takes so much work to keep me on track. Will life get easier? Will I have peace for any length of time?*

In the end, I learned all I could do was take life one day at a time and hold onto my faith that someday I'd feel stable and normal. Have you been able to hold onto hope for your own healing? Do you ask yourself similar questions?

At times, my emotional intensity was so strong that I needed time alone away from my family. I felt jumpy and disturbed. If I could, I would ask my husband to watch the children and I would drive to an empty church parking lot nearby. It was usually at night, and I would take my journal. The lot faced a pond with a little island and a lit-up statue that I found comforting. I would let myself go into a wailing cry or yell out or just sit motionless for a while. Eventually, I would journal about what was happening, and sometimes a vision would follow. Then I would go home in an exhausted, yet somewhat lighter state, and go to sleep. In the journal entry below, I tried to remember that there was a healthy part of me that knew all I was going through was happening for a reason, for growth, but that I needed help.

I'm powerful, and I will fight for my life and for my family. I will do what I have to do, and I'll heal. My ADS will be okay.

Then my ADS responded with more anger toward me.

I asked her, "Who are you really mad at?"

And she replied, "Me, myself."

I asked Jesus to please comfort and help her. I told her, "I know you feel you can't let your guard down, you need your armor, it's too scary for you to feel your pain, the wounds are devastating, and vulnerability isn't safe."

My ADS said she scares herself.

My AS responded, "I hear how afraid you are, and I'm here with you. I love you even if you can't love yourself. I will hold you when you think no one will. I will hold hope for you when you have none. I believe in you, ADS. I believe in your strength, your insight, and your heart. I know there is love in you. I know it."

When her pain was on the surface, those were usually times that I wasn't doing well.

My level of functioning is going downhill. I'm moving in slow motion again and giving up on trying to function. I'm in the bed again, and it feels like I'm hanging on by a thread. Between me and a drink, smoke, and food is a thread. Between me and insanity is a thread. Between me and death is a thread. I can't sleep, even though I'm exhausted. I keep asking Jesus to help me and asking Him what I should do next. No one call me or come see me; I'm not fit.

I'm at a crossroads. Who do I choose—God or the devil/fear mind? It feels like that point of no return when the fight to heal gets beaten down for the last time.

After journaling, I had a vision:

The dark one circles around me once again. I can feel his energy sucking the life out of me and offering addiction. I cry out for Jesus's help, and He lifts my limp body off the rocks, all cracked and bloodied, and carries me off with His beautiful Grace. I finally know my only peace, my only solace, my only real hope is in His arms. Let my ADS's rage die. I rest beside still waters by His side in the valley of darkness. I rest by Him. He carries me, He holds me, He never ever leaves me. I follow Him. My ADS takes her armor off in Jesus's presence for the first time. She allows Him to see her devastation. Her entire body is an open wound, just a mass of bloody flesh. Then she crawls into one of Jesus's wounds. It is the only place she feels safe. How appropriate for this wounded part of me to crawl into one of Jesus's most vulnerable places—His wound.

The days following this vision, I came upon the Anima Christi prayer. I had been going through a bunch of Catholic prayer pamphlets I had stashed away in a drawer by my altar; I'd never had the time to read them before. The prayer amazed me because it contained imagery about going into Jesus's wounds just like I saw in my vision.

That blew my mind! I thought it was odd how my younger parts went into his wound, until I realized it made sense for my most vulnerable parts to go into His for safety. Over the next several months, there were many visits to His wounds.

ANIMA CHRISTI

Soul of Christ, sanctify me.
Body of Christ, save me.
Blood of Christ, inebriate me.
Water from Christ's side, wash me.
Passion of Christ, strengthen me.
O good Jesus, hear me.
Within Thy wounds hide me.
Suffer me not to be separated from Thee.
From the malicious enemy defend me.
In the hour of my death call me.
And bid me come unto Thee,
That I may praise Thee with Thy saints
And with Thy angels,
Forever and ever.
Amen.

What a rough time! I was afraid I would hurt myself and almost checked myself into the hospital for fear of completely losing control and committing suicide. Suicidal ideation is not a good sign but an understandable one, considering what survivors go through. It just felt like my pain would never end. I was so afraid that I would keep fighting only to find out that I was too broken to fix and would have to let go of my dreams of healing peace. My wonderful SAC just kept *bringing me back to the present and reminding me to take one day at a time, one moment at a time, and that it wouldn't remain this hard.* She held hope for me when I couldn't. This is why it's so important to me to write my story for those of you who really can't see an end to your torment. You'll see as we move further into my story that I'm living proof that the torment lessens, and the peace increases when you keep striving to heal. There is hope for you to heal, and I'm holding out hope for you right now. Each step we take toward our healing creates a stronger base, so that when new phases or times of difficulty knock on our door, we meet them from a stronger place than we could in the past. We do reap benefits along the way and not just on the other side of our healing.

* * *

At this point in time, I was forty-five years old and still in the crisis phase. There was so much healing work going on that it seemed to be all I was doing. I guess once I opened the door, there was no going back, as it just kept coming at me. I did understand it was helping me though, so I wasn't trying to stop it. One day at home alone while the kids were at school, my ICW continued. My inner child parts needed revenge for what had been done to them! As I sat on my bed feeling small and overwhelmed with multiple intense emotions all at once, I experienced the following vision.

> *I close my eyes to meditate, but I see my ADS standing there holding a long-handled axe. Oh no! Then I see all the younger parts of myself lined up in the middle of the road where I grew up, each with a weapon except my baby self. Damn! My AS has my baby self in a sling and asks Archangel Michael to protect us. We march up the road to the neighborhood rapist's house and drag him out into his yard. My ADS wields her axe like a true warrior and plants it right between his eyes. See ya, bastard!*

This symbolized what my younger selves felt had been done to them. Kids think in a concrete physical sense rather than an abstract emotional sense. Even though that vision was gruesome, it marked an important turning point in my healing journey. My younger selves finally had some sense of justice. They were able to release rage from that time in their life, take action—*no longer lying there and taking it while being raped and betrayed.* Now, my younger self was the one with the power and control, as in the "I, Warrior" vision. Meanwhile, my AS understood that my older self had a different need, and that was to forgive. I needed to forgive everything that was done to me, from any layer or aspect I could think of. But that was a very gradual process that occurred naturally as I healed. Forgiveness is an expression of love that releases the grip of events and others' hold on me. All true permanent healing occurs through love.

Then a healing vision appeared in my mind. A welcome relief to have something positive.

> *All of my younger selves plus my AS are walking up my current driveway together. As we walk, my AS tells my younger selves where we live, and I tell them our current address. I tell them I'm married to a good man, I'm forty-five years old now, I have two wonderful loving children, and we live in a safe home. All of my different age selves are distinct, yet we are one. I see all of my younger parts go into my AS and become one as we walk up my driveway together as one united front. We are safe and we are free.*

I knew this was huge in the healing department and was deeply moved by it. I was integrating and becoming whole, but like many other experiences with healing, it was only a taste of what was to come. I would still revisit my pain; I had more work to do.

If you had told me how long all this healing work was going to take, I would have told you that you are nuts! TOO LONG! We must try to remember that our healing occurs one step at a time and we reap the benefits throughout our journey. We slowly feel better because it doesn't happen all at once for most of us. Thankfully, there are trauma re-processing therapies like EMDR, Somatic Experiencing, and Brain Spotting now available. I believe these tools would have moved my healing along at a much faster pace if I'd had access to them. Up until the two-year crisis phase, my healing work was spread out and more manageable. Two years is nothing though, compared to the many years I'll be blessed from the time and energy spent doing this intense healing work.

* * *

I revisit boundary work frequently since it's a critical part of recovery. I continued to work on boundaries and setting limits with others by listening to my needs and not what others told me I need. For example, many times I just needed to be in comfy clothes, lying safely in my bed instead of being at an AA meeting. My sponsor did not understand this, but I held my ground. What I needed was so clear to me, and it was empowering to stick up for what I knew felt right for my own healing. I knew when I needed a meeting, and I would go at those times.

Boundary and codependency work were signs of progress. I'd write down questions to ask myself in different situations like: "Do I want to do this? Am I taking care of myself? Remember, I have the right to take care of myself." I had to remember that self-care is *healthy*, and all those I interact with benefit when I take care of myself. It was also important to model healthy self-care behavior for others, especially my children. I kept working on keeping myself separately from others, remembering to do my stuff and let others do theirs.

Part of my healing included telling my mother about my trauma. I was starting to be able to hold all of my conflicting feelings about her at one time instead of compartmentalizing them. However, I needed to have a defined sense of self before I told her, and I had to know where I started and ended—another reason the boundary and codependency work was essential.

I began thinking I would confront her. That approach was coming from my younger selves, but that isn't how it happened in the end. I didn't feel the same need to confront my attackers because I knew they were sick and I had no expectations for them to be protective and loving. For those of you who are survivors of incest, I know you have more consuming layers of betrayal, confusion, and pain. Your abuser was most likely someone you loved and trusted, someone who was supposed to be protecting you. Those of you who have been abducted, you also have more layers of pain. I pray for you to get the help you deserve in order to heal from your devastating wounds.

* * *

My dear husband stood by me; he loved and supported me every step of the way. I'm grateful to him, and I thank God often for blessing me with such a beautiful man. My husband has taught me many lessons about trust, loyalty, boundaries, priorities, how to be part of a family, and best of all, love. I didn't go into rape details with him because it's too difficult for him. So, I respected *his* boundaries. I love him with all my heart.

I want to share this beautiful vision with you I call "The Golden

Lotus." It shows how my inner mental terrain was shifting to a more positive place during this phase of healing.

> *I see Kwan Yin, the Goddess of Mercy, standing on the ocean. I see her beautiful face; her robes are blowing in the wind, and pretty objects dangle in her gorgeous long black hair. I ask her if I can have a drop from her cup of compassion. It washes over me. I lie on the ocean, moving peacefully with the water. Kwan Yin reaches down and puts a lotus flower on my third eye, my heart, my pubic area, and on my spinal T6 and T7 areas. Then she puts an enormous open lotus flower under me. It holds me and keeps me safe while I rest on the water. She leaves. The lotus gently washes up on a beach. I thank her and send her loving gratitude.*

The Golden Lotus

The ocean waves gently flow under her feet
Her robes wisp in the sea air
Her beautiful face, her flowing black hair

She is the Goddess of Mercy
The Mother of love and compassion
The Sacred Lotus Flower

She pours a drop from her cup of infinite compassion
It washes over me like a blanket of love
She covers my wounds with lotus flowers
And places me in a sacred lotus boat

She is Kwan Yin
The Golden Lotus

****

In the second year of my crisis phase, just when I began to have longer breaks from my emotional intensity—I even went out to see some friends and wasn't in bed as much—I began to struggle again with suicidal thinking. How could I have such dark thoughts when things were just starting to look up? I woke up one morning after dreaming about wanting to die and just letting go.

At that point, I had a paramount realization: I'm sad and exhausted, not suicidal. I needed to rest, not let go of life. That same day while driving home from dropping my children off at school, I kept having disturbing thoughts like, *I could just stop breathing. I could just drive into that tree.* After pulling into the garage, I thought, *I could just sit here and let the car run*. I addressed these thoughts because I knew not to let them go without acknowledgment. So, I reminded myself that I just needed to take it easy while I was in such distress. I didn't truly want to die; I wanted to be here for my family.

I allowed myself to feel the sadness that fueled my suicidal thoughts. Sadness over the loss of freedom a child has knowing when they feel protected. The loss of my childhood set in more deeply. I sank into a river of sorrow and cried at home to release my grief.

I tried so hard to accept my sadness, where I was on my path, and the truth that I wasn't getting worse. There were many days I saw myself in my mind's eye shuffling behind Jesus while holding onto his robe as he led me through the valley. He was such a comfort to me, and I know He carried me through my pain. Here's a beautiful prayer based on the popular poem *Footprints in the Sand* to remind us we are not alone with our pain. Even when we think no one is there, we are never alone.

The Footprints Prayer

One night I had a dream ...

I dreamed I was walking along the beach with the Lord, and across the sky flashed scenes from my life. For each scene I noticed two sets of footprints in the sand; one belonged to me, and the other to the Lord. When the last scene of my life flashed before us, I looked back at the footprints in the sand. I noticed that many times along the path of my life, there was only one set of footprints.

I also noticed that it happened at the very lowest and saddest times in my life. This really bothered me, and I questioned the Lord about it. "Lord, you said that once I decided to follow You, You would walk with me all the way. But I have noticed that during the most troublesome times in my life, there is only one set of footprints. I don't understand why in times when I needed you the most, you should leave me."

The Lord replied, "My precious, precious child. I love you, and I would never, never leave you during your times of trial and suffering. When you saw only one set of footprints, it was then that I carried you."

That prayer is what I experienced.

My dreams started to change at this point in my healing too. They were showing me progress and providing insight. In them, I fought like hell and chased some of the rapists off. How about that! I also had dreams of how confused I was about being female and afraid to look good because some man might attack me. The dream below was a new one for me:

> *I am bathing in a hotel, and there are blood fragments everywhere, all over the floor and in the surrounding rooms. I want to join a group to socialize, eat, and have fun, but I keep telling myself I have to clean up the blood first. I am cleaning and sobbing and saying, "I hate this! I hate this! I hate this so much!" By the time I go to join the group, both they and the food are gone. Then I try to meet up with them at the pool, but I get lost and end up at the beach, and there is no flood this time.*

My interpretation of that dream is that the crisis phase was a bloody mess, and I hated that I had to work through so much. I missed out on things since I wasn't up to socializing for quite a while. I had no desire to because I was exhausted and consumed with the bloody mess that I knew only I could clean up for myself. But, in the dream, I did clean up my trauma mess, so that's a positive. There was no flood at the beach in this dream because the flood of repressed emotion was slowly releasing.

* * *

Wow, the crisis phase was finally ending! When I reflect on this phase, I just cringe at the seemingly unending damage sexual trauma causes. Horrific events occur, and many survivors go through such terrible darkness. It's hard to believe that anyone is put through this hell, especially a child.

I feel the following poem captures the relentless nature of the damage caused by being sexually assaulted as a child.

Insidious

It lurks in every cell of my being
This insidious disease.
I hear words like victim, trauma, and sexual assault.
I sleep with it, eat with it, love with it,
Numb with it, cry, rage, and die with it.
Everything I see, I hear, I feel, I touch,
Is filtered through this insidious disease.
I cower, I sink, I drown, I rot with it.
There is nowhere to run or hide from it.
NO SAFE PLACE EXCEPT GOD.
I accept the truth of who I am.
I accept the rage, the endless gut-wrenching pain.
I accept, I accept, I accept
This insidious disease.
And then, I move on in peace.

****

Patti said that I was not the insidious disease, but rather, society is. It isn't that there is something wrong with me. In reality, it's a cultural problem of sick adults and teens sexually assaulting children. It's a systemic issue, and we need healthy adult role models taking a stand and teaching our young about this issue.

I felt I needed to lay out the details of my inner experience as a survivor because it's the truth I lived. My childhood trauma was being seen, processed, released, and forgiven, one step at a time. No more haunting me from the hidden depths of my mind. I was moving at a tremendous pace in the last year of my crisis phase. The healing work I was doing on my own and with my SAC was moving my trauma from my primitive brain (amygdala), where traumatic events are stored, to my rational brain (cerebral cortex) where I could work with it (see Appendix D, Trauma Education and Triggers).

The crisis phase lasted a little over two years, and then I started to get stronger and stronger. It was time to work on telling my mother about being raped as a child. Telling anyone, especially family members, is difficult, since a lot is at stake, like being rejected, blamed, disbelieved, or cut off. I hope the next chapter, in which I describe telling my mother about my trauma, is of help to you if you're contemplating telling someone in your own life.

Telling Mother My Secrets

(45–46 years old)

During this time, I was still experiencing flashbacks and visual memories for the first time since the rapes occurred. As I prepared to tell my mother, I learned some information about telling abuse secrets that helped give me confidence. In the book I earlier referred to as my healing bible, *The Courage to Heal*, there is an insightful list of why survivors need to tell their secrets. Following are a lead-in quote from the book and a list of reasons to tell.

"Survivors have also been blamed, ridiculed, or shunned. Yet in spite of these negative experiences from the past, it is necessary to take a leap of faith and tell."[27] (**Note:** I added references for men in parentheses.)

WHY TELLING IS TRANSFORMATIVE

- You move through the shame and secrecy that keeps you isolated.
- You move through denial and acknowledge the truth of your abuse.

---

27 Ellen Bass and Lauren Davis, *The Courage to Heal: A Guide for Women Survivors of Childhood Sexual Abuse*, 3rd ed. (New York: Harper Collins, 1994), 106.

- You make it possible to get understanding and help.
- You get more in touch with your feelings.
- You get a chance to see your experience (and yourself) through the compassionate eyes of a supporter.
- You make space in relationships for the kind of intimacy that comes from honesty.
- You establish yourself as a person in the present who is dealing with the abuse in her (or his) past.
- You join a courageous community of women who are no longer willing to suffer in silence. (*The Courage to Heal* book was written for women. Men, you will join a courageous community of men who are no longer willing to suffer in silence.)
- You help end child sexual abuse by breaking the silence in which it thrives.
- You become a model for other survivors.
- You (eventually) feel proud and strong.[28]

I love that book, and it helped me understand why I needed to tell my mother.

Another reason it was important to tell my mother was that I had been trying to forgive her for many years and couldn't understand why it just wouldn't happen. I wanted to have peace with her before she left this earth. I hoped to accept my mother as best I could while she is here but found I couldn't until I told her the truth. We had to face it together even though I knew how painful and possibly destructive it could be for us.

28 Bass and Davis, *The Courage to Heal*, 106.

My AS wanted to protect my mother from this pain. My child self feared it would physically kill her to know the truth, or it would kill our relationship. A big piece of being stuck was that my younger self wanted my mother to know what happened, like any child would. I just couldn't bear holding the secrets anymore. If I was ever going to be able to move on, I had to let go and tell. I prayed that something good would come out of telling her, instead of just causing more pain.

It was important that I took my time to work out what I would tell my mother and waited until I felt strong and safe enough to do so. Telling was supposed to be about healing, not re-victimizing myself or assigning blame to my mother. This was not something to rush into, and I knew I would know when I was ready. One of the first preparation tools I used was to come up with a list of positives and negatives about telling her. There were several more positives than negatives.

Patti asked me if telling my mother became too much for my younger selves to handle, would my AS be ready to protect them. As the adult, I needed to prove to my younger selves that I could and would be their protector. The more I proved I could keep my younger selves safe by holding strong boundaries, the more they trusted and quieted down. That led to me being able to live my life as an adult, instead of frequently having my injured child self on the surface unconsciously running the show. But mostly, I realized that telling my mother was about making peace inside me, as well as between me and her. Is there someone you need to tell about your trauma? If so, I hope you take your time preparing and protecting yourself as much as possible from their possible negative reactions.

I planned to write my mother a letter, and then once it was finished,

Patti was going to help me decide whether to read it to her in person or over the phone, or just send it to her. Taking time to review my options with Patti was comforting, and it gave me time to get some clarity from my wise inner self. I didn't have to figure it out all by myself. I originally wanted to read it to my mother in a session with Patti, but I realized that my mother could refuse to come and that might leave me wide open for more pain. My CS needed to be closely monitored throughout this process, so my AS made decisions based on what would feel safest for me.

During one of my sessions, Patti and I explored whether I had the right to hurt my mother in order to help myself. I told Patti that I knew telling was not about wanting to hurt my mother, and I hoped it would have a healing effect on us both. It had been hurting me for most of my forty-five years and was the never-disappearing elephant in my life. My mother had been off the hook all these years while I suffered with it, and now I needed to tell her. I'm sure there will be those people who say, "Oh, forgive and forget." Where does that leave me? Let's see, make the victim handle it by herself, she holds it all and stays stuck indefinitely. Nope, I wasn't letting it happen that way!

I began witnessing my rebirth. From all the work I had done thus far, it was coming together and showing up in the way I saw myself as an individual, and owned who I was by telling my mother the truth. I also wasn't letting others influence me so much. I could tell her now. I was finding my voice and learning how to own my power and follow my gut. It felt great. It felt empowering.

* * *

The healing process was such a roller coaster of breaking apart and getting stronger, then falling apart again. I would take a few steps forward and a couple back.

In order to prepare for the likelihood that this would be another setback experience, I reached out to my hypnotherapist for some extra support. He talked to me about forgiveness and cutting the rapists' hold on me. He talked about how rage does not give me power, it gives the rapists' power. During this session, while I was being hypnotized in the recliner chair, I saw Archangel Michael in my mind. He held my face with his hands and looked into my eyes and said, "Love yourself like we [the Holy Ones] love you." I felt so much love; tears rolled down my cheeks. I felt lighter and good. Yes, I do deserve to be loved. I'm so grateful.

Note: Please take this in. When we hate and rage at our abuser or anyone else, we give them power over us. We are allowing them to control our feelings, thoughts, and behaviors. When we forgive, we take our power back. Hatred is fear-based and weakens us, whereas love and forgiveness give us strength. When we feed ourselves with love and forgiveness, I believe we progress faster. Watch what you focus on, like the American Indian saying says below.

One evening an old Cherokee told his grandson
About a battle that goes on inside people.

He said, "My son, the battle is between
two 'wolves' inside us all."

One is evil.
It is anger, envy, jealousy, sorrow, regret, greed,
Arrogance, self-pity, guilt, resentment, inferiority, lies,

False pride, superiority, and ego.

The other is good.
It is joy, peace, love, hope, serenity, humility,
kindness, benevolence,
Empathy, generosity, truth, compassion, and faith.

The grandson thought about it for a minute
And then asked his grandfather,
"Which wolf wins?"

The old Cherokee simply replied,
"The one you feed."

—A Cherokee parable

Hypnotherapy and meeting with Patti helped me feed the loving wolf within me. So did reaching out to my husband, who kept calling to check on me during particularly difficult days. On one occasion, I was limp in my bed once again in a clinical depression. He offered to bring me to a bed and breakfast for a weekend and made me feel so loved and supported. It's our favorite place to go together, and it's nestled in a park surrounded by trees and wildlife. The breakfasts there are just scrumptious with homemade goods and fresh-squeezed orange juice. As you sit to eat, you can watch all the pretty birds on a feeder just outside a big picture window. We spent a quiet weekend there where I could cry, rest, and move like a snail in slow motion. I could only take in small bits of information and function on a limited scale. It felt comforting to me to feel seen and taken care of.

Hope and self-love were outside me, and when I did manage to hold them, they would fly away easily. I hadn't internalized them yet, but Patti and loved ones helped hold them for me. I could love others, but self-love was difficult. Chaos was more familiar. I continued the work of simplifying my life and focused on self-care and structure. This was part of my strengthening phase of recovery. I designated special days for me to do whatever I wanted and try to do something comforting. It felt liberating to wake up on my designated special day of the week and ask myself, "Marie, what would feel most comforting for you to do while the kids are at school today?" I didn't have to be in crisis to get in my bed because I gave myself permission to extend kindness to myself. I was learning how to love myself step-by-step as expressed in the journal entry below:

> *I see myself growing—loving myself more and more deeply each day, giving myself permission to do beautiful things for me. I have a voice, I can say no. Today is my day and I get to do whatever I want, which is usually getting snuggled in bed all cozied up. I feel like I need a lifetime of comfort. I don't feel guilty for this time in bed, for this beautiful gift I give myself. I'm worth it, I deserve it, and I'm valuable.*

Patti said, "Nothing you ever do for yourself is a waste." I was seeing more progress watching a woman emerging as my developmentally arrested younger parts quieted down, and I was connecting to my AS instead of letting my younger parts run the show.

One of the things that ate at me during the crisis phase was feeling like a burden to my husband. When I told him about that, he said, "Maybe that's why I'm here, to take care of you." What a gift he is. I'm grateful, and I love him very much. Patti noticed how my husband gave me room to grow and provided a safe environment to do my inner work. He allowed me to go wherever I needed to go and didn't get defensive or project his "stuff" onto me. She described him as the poster man or the model healthy man. She's absolutely right!

One of the ways my husband was supportive was when he agreed to come to a therapy session with me. He finally got to meet Patti! She and I had talked about how hard it is for a survivor's spouse. We wanted a space for him to ask any questions and for Patti to explain about healing from trauma. I was so nervous, having never been to therapy with another person before. It just felt odd having another person in the room. We talked about my journey, the hardships for my husband living with me, and my current struggles. She explained to him that I would move into a more stable healing place after I'd worked through whatever needed to be addressed. It meant so much to me that he was willing to join us. The session was very helpful.

With support, healing work, and growth, I started to see more positive shifts in my level of functioning as reflected in the journal entry below.

> *I'm starting to see that I'm pulling my weight, and my marriage isn't as lopsided. I cook, clean, do errands, and most importantly, take wonderful care of myself and our children. I love being a mother, and when I'm feeling well, it's the tops. I love my husband and take care of him too. I'm learning how to relax, how to be peaceful, how to love myself, how to give myself understanding and patience, and to make allowances for rest, exercise, and fun so I can blossom. My priorities are God, self, and family first. I'm letting go of shame. Wow, I really can* **love myself! What a gift***!*

I continued getting stronger and feeling better equipped to handle my visits to the valley of pain and darkness. One day I was taking a healing bath, soaking in the warmth of the water that comforted my feeling broken and small. I would have this open wound feeling, as I've mentioned before, and a feeling of my insides being broken glass. It was disturbing, to say the least. I asked Jesus to help me rebirth myself. I walked into His wound that my younger selves hid in for safety and love. As I walked, my younger selves were on either side of me, weeping over my pain as they followed me in and then surrounded me. I could feel their strength and love. I realized how I first needed to know their truth of what happened to them and how they felt. Now, I was learning the truth about my AS, who I really am, and what I can realistically do.

After my bath, I decided to look at my groin area because I had discomfort there. Unfortunately, I found two tiny ticks embedded—this was a week after hiking off-trail at a beautiful park nearby. I had done my tick check, but those ticks were elusive due to their tiny size and hidden location. I was feeling seriously sick and knew something was wrong with me. I went to see my physician a couple of times, and he could see how I was going downhill. My blood test for Lyme disease came back negative. Since I had been bitten, he decided to treat me for one month and no more, as the medical guidelines dictated. However, after the one month ended, I was still very symptomatic. I prayed for help while researching what was wrong with me on the Internet, and I concluded it was Lyme disease, despite the negative test result. After researching for hours and reading many technical articles, I concluded that one month of treatment wasn't going to resolve my symptoms. I found a Lyme-Literate MD (LLMD) who ruled out what he could through medical testing and used a clinical diagnosis to determine if I had Lyme disease. He diagnosed me with multiple tick-born diseases, and we began a long journey of treatment.

After more time taking antibiotics, I was up and around, and the shooting pains and achiness stopped. The last symptoms to show up were the first to leave. Over the next year and a half, I took multiple antibiotics, zeroing in on different tick-borne diseases until my body couldn't tolerate the medication anymore. I then took herbal treatments for another year until I was symptom free.

The standard six weeks of treatment was a complete joke. Thank God I didn't listen to conventional treatment, which is based on politics and money. It doesn't give a damn about the individual suffering with tick-borne diseases. And by the way, Lyme blood test results cannot be trusted. I had a clinical diagnosis based on my history, symptom picture, and ruling out other diseases. My LLMD watched how well I responded to Lyme treatment, and we knew we were on the right track. He believed I had Lyme disease for a long time and then was re-infected.

While I was very sick, my LLMD referred me to a very special lady named Angela Dumas, who is a spiritual health coach (SHC) and someone who had suffered greatly at the hand of Lyme disease. My doctor said he had numerous patients that progressed faster while working with her. I called her and worked with her for a couple of years. She turned out to be a major support for my trauma too!

One day while feeling beaten down from my healing journey and needing help with holding hope, I emailed Angela:

> *I have to ask you a question. Can you string days, weeks, or even months together where you feel okay and can carry out your responsibilities—live your life without torment? I haven't been able to yet. I just need to know, is there really hope for me? Will life always*

be this hard? Will I ever stop grasping for the next cure that will hopefully give me peace?

She lovingly responded with hope, just as Patti did when I would ask her the same questions, and I was grateful for their encouragement. Angela midwifed me through some awful periods right along with Patti. I felt I could handle anything with the loving support of my husband, children, and these two powerful women. Both women came from an empowerment frame of reference, and that was exactly what I needed. They encouraged me, educated me, and taught me coping tools, witnessed my pain, and provided a safe and loving space for me to heal. As time went on, I felt more and more capable of handling my trauma responses on my own, because I was internalizing what they had taught me.

* * *

When I was still forty-five, the next flashback happened while I was alone at home. It was from the gang rape attack, and it was followed by this comforting vision that occurred while I was praying. Here's an entry from my journal.

I was reciting the prayers honoring the Seven Sorrows of the Virgin Mary when halfway through I had a vision. I was suddenly a young teen squatting by the side of the house where I had been gang raped by three teen boys. I was trance-like, dazed, and disoriented, had already forgotten being raped, and was trying to get myself up to walk home. The feeling of loneliness and devastation was unbearable. The Virgin Mary appeared and bent down to help me up. She didn't say a word while she quietly walked me home. It felt incredibly comforting for someone, anyone, no less the Virgin Mary, to help me not feel alone with my pain. It felt alien to be comforted, but I felt lifted up by her presence. During the days after the vision, every time I thought of her loving presence, I cried.

I believe she walked me home on the actual day of the rape too. How would I ever have made it through my journey without God and those who represent Him? I just don't see how I could have done it without them. Do you feel supported through your own spiritual connections? Feelings of shame and unworthiness can act as a block to being able to open to, and aware of, God's loving presence. Being abused in the name of God, as many have sadly experienced, also acts as a block from opening to a Divine presence. Just because one may be unintentionally blocking spiritual presence, doesn't mean it isn't there.

Later that month, after a heavy session with my SHC, I had started some necessary work with my younger selves, which left me feeling sad and angry. Angela helped me open up to more work I needed to do during one of our calls, and then afterward, I would continue healing work on my own in my bedroom. I saw in my mind's eye the following healing vision about self-empowerment.

My dead-looking preschool self is lying on the ground, and my ADS is standing by her, screaming mad. She is enraged over the adults in her life failing to recognize that there was something wrong and failing to protect her. Now all of my younger parts are lying lifeless on the ground at my AS's feet. My AS cries out over the carnage, the damage in the wake of rape. My AS carries my younger selves one by one into Jesus's wound, where I lay them down, kiss their foreheads, and say, "You are healing here. You are safe and protected. No one will hurt you."

My AS talks to my baby, toddler/preschool, school age, adolescent, and teen selves. "Are we going to let the pedophiles, society, and parental failures define us? Are we going to let their ignorance, denial, and ineptness take us down? Each one of you survived so that the next older one could live. Each one of you has insight, wisdom, courage, and passion—priceless experience and knowledge that could help other survivors. Are we going to let our pain and rage control us after all we have fought through and survived? Or are we going to harness that powerful energy and passion from our pain and be warriors for other children and comfort for other survivors—the walking wounded like us?

"The answer is yes! When you put together what each of us has to offer, I know we can help someone. We can know good came from our suffering." As my AS is talking, my younger parts slowly wake up and start nodding in agreement. I continue:

"We are one, we support each other, and we are strong."

It was great how we were an allied group and becoming one. My younger parts needed my AS to keep setting limits, guiding, and protecting—in other words, re-parenting them. The re-parenting and integration work were paramount in propelling my healing progress.

* * *

I had just gotten home from therapy with Patti and sat down on my porch to process the session. I was spending an increased amount of time in more positive mental and emotional states, but there were still times when I reverted back to my old self-judgmental behavior. I noticed that I would get exasperated with keeping myself on track because it was so much work.

Patti provided supportive thoughts, and then I journaled them in my words. She helped me tune into myself and honor what I wanted. It was a practice of learning that I mattered and knowing how to reach myself. Angela, my SHC, was also introducing me to many new techniques for my healing toolbox. The Emotional Freedom Technique (EFT) was one I had tried and liked in the past, and I was glad that she also used it. EFT uses a tapping motion on certain energetic points on the body while you say certain phrases. The point is to unblock trapped energy, and it works especially well on blocked trauma. The website for this appears in Appendix A, Helpful Resources.

I contacted Angela numerous times in crisis (usually emotional), and she would get right back to me, eager to help. Her loving presence alone was healing. It was truly amazing how she would turn me around, usually right away or within a day. I'm grateful to her. I was improving with her help and just one month after working with her, I strung together six days without a negatively intense mood. Yes! Oh my gosh, it was happening. There really is hope for me, and I don't have to endure suffering the rest of my life with trauma pain.

* * *

The vacillating back and forth between feeling okay and then not, continued. As my birthday approached, my mother's visit, along with some other events, triggered another intense state. Feeling the need to tell her came to the surface again. I journaled the following.

> *It's my 46th birthday. Several events in the last day have triggered a build-up of anxiety. My mother is visiting, my friend is talking about a possible local pedophile, there was a disturbing incident at my children's school involving a female student that was presenting*

with what I thought were symptoms of abuse, and there is another story about child abuse on the TV that I can't seem to turn off. I feel overwhelmed by all the **triggers** *today. It's late at night and I'm in the bathroom sobbing. Eventually I go to bed and try to go to sleep when my husband hears me sobbing in bed. All I can remember saying to him was, "the pain, the pain, it hurts so badly." My husband, who rarely gives advice with my emotional issues, tells me he feels I need to tell my mother and just let it out. He suggests a letter.*

It's three days later, and my mother is leaving. I have a minor case of asthma, but it's not minor now. My lungs feel so tight and heavy, and my mood is sad and angry. I need to tell her, but I'm scared of the outcome. I don't want to cause her pain, yet the need to tell her is consuming me. It sits on me, and I carry it wherever I go. It just won't go away. What's the source of this relentless need to tell her? I've told other people, but none of it matters like telling her—I want my mommy to know!

I can see a wall or block within me that symbolizes her not knowing. Can I tell and not take responsibility for her reaction, her pain? What she does with that information is not my responsibility. Can I accept that I have a need to tell my mom what happened to me? Relief.

Nothing ever goes away until it has taught us what we need to know.

—Pema Chödrön[29]

Later the next day, I read a Lenten Reflection pamphlet I had picked up at church titled "The Commitment Move," and part of it read,

29 "Pema Chödrön Quotes," goodreads, accessed January 17, 2018, https://www.goodreads.com/quotes/593844-nothing-ever-goes-away-until-it-has-taught-us-what.

"Trust enough to make the commitment move. Is there a next step you should take in bridging an estranged relationship or *correcting a difficult situation that you are hesitant to commit to*? Trusting in your word, may we dare to walk the difficult trail of justice and forgiveness so that we may one day make our way to the place where you dwell forever?" Can you believe that? Talk about a clear message from God. I knew it, my husband knew it, Patti and Angela knew it, and God knew it. It was time to commit to telling, and I was ready. I finally wrote the letter to my mother and planned to review it with my SAC the next day.

Patti said my letter was factual, using "I" statements, it wasn't harsh or attacking, and I wasn't trying to take care of my mother—just stating the events and my feelings. I started the letter with, "I need to tell you about some things that I have been through." I talked about flashbacks and general facts about my rapes. I decided to send a copy of it to my sisters first, so they knew what my mother was about to read and reminded them that Mom should come to me with her questions and reactions. I suggested they not try to speak for me. My sisters were supportive and loving, and I am so grateful. Their support was exactly what I needed.

During this getting-ready-to-tell process, my younger selves were right on the surface and full of fear. Especially my toddler/preschool self, who was convinced my mother would drop dead when she read the letter. She was expressing her childhood magical thinking, or maybe she was right. DAMN! Could she be right?

During the session with, Patti, my young child self's fears were evident, so I asked Patti if my mother would die. Patti explained that the rapists threatened me and my family if I told. So, of course, my

CS would think my mom might die. Patti went on to say that my mom was a grownup and had been through many things. She could handle it. It was her responsibility to handle what she was told. Patti told my younger self that it was okay to tell and that my AS would protect her. My AS kept reassuring my younger selves and watching my boundaries as needed. The telling process became an opportunity to support myself, and it felt scary, yet empowering.

Patti walked me through each and every piece of this and many other processes as I healed. She did it with expertise, grace, and love. I'm grateful and appreciate every ounce of herself she put into helping me.

I was experiencing moments at home when I distinctly smelled my father's cologne, or my grandmother's perfume, as I was walking down the hall or stood in the kitchen. They had both passed away years earlier, and I yearned for their company while I struggled. They were with me in spirit, supporting me the best they could. I sensed their concern and desire to have been able to protect me when I was a child. I love my father and grandmother dearly and was comforted by their presence.

Soon after a visit with Patti, I had a dream about my dad riding a horse around the outskirts of my protective corral, the corral that I visualize to feel safe and build up my personal boundaries. I was so glad to see him in my dream and really felt his support, so I added him to my corral imagery from then on. Sometimes my CS would invite him in our round hobbit-like safety hut at the center of the corral, where he would snuggle with me amongst lots of big mushy pillows and stuffed animals.

I reminisced about when one of my sisters and I moved in with him in my twenties; I was able to hang out and talk to him much more than when I was little. He gave me his full attention, and I felt loved and seen by him. We became very close.

My fear of telling was palpable at this point and I felt deeply vulnerable, and yet I felt so supported by my dad and grandmother. Patti kept reminding me to draw upon my prayer, meditation, and boundary tools because they helped keep me grounded and strong. My younger selves watched my AS like a hawk to see if I would stand up for myself and be protective. They identified with their victim place, and they were beginning to learn they could trust their adult self to care for them and keep them safe. This was huge for me, and I wanted to honor it. Telling my mother would be a test and a great opportunity for my growth and ability to thrive.

After reviewing the letter to my mother with Patti, I mailed it and waited, vacillating between weakness and strength. Can you fathom what it would be like to mail that letter or to receive it? My mother got the letter and called me in a devastated state. I immediately told my younger selves they could go where they felt safe, like in Jesus's wound or our safety hut, but they wanted to stay with me. My teen self was on one side, my adolescent on the other, and the rest were behind. Then my AS decided to picture us all in our corral as we listened. Patti warned me that parents' reactions commonly include being defensive and angry, and then hopefully move into support. Unfortunately, many won't be able to leave their denial in order to hear the painful truth.

My mother started off being defensive and angry, asking questions like: How could you drop this in my lap without details? Who raped you?

What neighborhood? Surprisingly, she moved quickly into support. I was shocked. She said she was so sorry for what happened to me, and she expressed total disbelief in how she could be so oblivious. How could she not have known something was wrong? She gave me baths, so how could she not have seen something? she asked. I explained that the preschool age rape was oral, and the others were when I was old enough to bathe myself. I told her I wasn't up for a grilling for information or to be put on the spot. We needed to take it slow, and she could come with me to sessions with my SAC to ask questions if she wanted. Yes, I set that safety boundary, and I didn't allow her to drag me or my precious younger parts over the blaming questions' coals.

At another point, I could see the conversation was going to a bad place of inferring blame for not telling her and shooting holes in my story, so I held my safety boundary and protected myself once again. It was so easy to go to my child victim place in that moment and just crumble. But I mustered up the strength to stand strong and take care of myself. My CS needed me. Letting my younger parts, or any part, get re-victimized was not allowed. I was proud that I could stand up for myself, and my younger selves were greatly relieved.

I kept reminding myself that her reactions were understandable and that she should be allowed to have her own responses, but they weren't mine. However, I did explain how kids rarely come out and tell their parents, and how I told her in other ways like not being able to walk suddenly, the hives episodes, self-medicating with alcohol at such a young age, etc. She questioned why I was angry with her for not protecting me when she didn't know. It's a complicated answer that I hope you have some understanding of after reading my story.

I think the biggest blow, other than her daughter being raped, was that her version of her mothering and my happy childhood got blown to pieces. She said, "I thought you had a great childhood, and now that's gone." It was a big loss for her.

Overall, her reaction was so much better than I thought it would be. Her apology and acknowledgment of what happened to me were exactly what my younger selves needed to hear. It was as though an angel whispered in her ear, "This is what your daughter needs to hear you say." She did well, considering the devastating news she had just received.

After speaking with my mom, I wrote this to my younger selves:

> *It's my responsibility to care for you. I protect us, call in help, and keep our boundaries strong. We will no longer mother Mom or take on her pain. We have enough of our own. She's an adult, and she will do what she'll do, as she always has. She'll probably vacillate between defense, denial, anger, and support. She must do this on her own. What we can do is pray for her to get the support she needs and to move through her pain as gracefully as possible.*

As soon as I could, I called Patti and described my mother's reaction. Patti explained that Mom's reaction was understandable shock and disbelief, which is a form of denial that protects by defending the mind. Soon after talking with my mom about my letter, I got a very special card from her:

> *… the most tragic event in my life was finding out that my daughter had her childhood stolen from her by violent sexual abuse. It is a miracle that you were not physically maimed or killed, and that you never took your own life, and that you became an amazing woman,*

a wonderful wife, and a mother with a beautiful family and many caring friends. God bless you. Love, Mom.

Oh my gosh, that meant so much to me! She did understand, and she lived through learning the truth, and we have a relationship today that is stronger than ever before. She stepped up to the mommy plate and supported me. Thank you, Mom—your reaction was healing.

After receiving my letter, she and I had several phone conversations where we went over different aspects of what we were each dealing with. I was cautious not to allow myself to get too vulnerable. She had been watching programs that talked about child rape and sharing what she learned with me. I felt seen, which was healing, and as a result, I placed less blame on my mother. Another result of telling her about my trauma was my pronounced healing growth and progress with forgiving, which were truly precious gifts. I could feel my relief and the removal of another healing block after telling her. I know so many survivors never get a supportive response from their family, and that saddens me. Have you been in the position of feeling a need to tell? If so, I hope you did, and I hope you were supported.

Another monumental outcome of telling my story was that it helped me find my voice and made me realize how important it was to feel heard. I had told my SAC, husband, some friends, my SHC, and my sisters, but the summit was telling my mother. My SAC helped me figure out that *telling shouldn't be about wanting something from her. It needed to be about my healing and helping me move forward.*

During my mother's first visit after the letter, I realized it was the best visit I could remember because there was a peace between us I hadn't felt before. Over time, my mother *appeared* to slip back into saying things that made me feel she was blaming me for being too trusting or oblivious, which I interpreted as her insinuating my rapes were my fault. She would recount how aware she was as a young person and would get out of bad situations right away because she had radar for problem situations and I did not. I believe she truly was perplexed by my broken radar or yuk-o-meter, and so am I.

What she was really doing was voicing her desperate need to find reasons why her daughter was repeatedly raped, and she was attempting to soothe her pain over failing to protect me. My mother had no awareness of, or intention to, blame me, but that was how I interpreted her comments through my own life filter. This was so painful for me. After going down emotionally several times, I decided to use my tools and forgive anyway, so my rage would not suffocate me more. The times when I was deeply hurt and angry, I chose not to defend myself from a place of anger because I knew I wasn't ready to address this situation with her yet. I believed if I did address it at that point, no healing would come from it. Something told me her comments weren't about me. When I was ready, I could witness her behavior without losing my peace because I would have a better understanding of the purpose of her comments.

This is partly how I addressed the situation once I felt ready. One day, after repeating the comments about me being too trusting on numerous occasions, I lovingly told her that when she said it that way, I felt like she was blaming me for being raped. She was shocked and felt bad about it. I told her that if she said it again I would leave the room because it hurt too much. My mother understood my interpretation of her comments and agreed to not discuss them anymore. Bringing her awareness to the issue without attacking her, but rather for helping us both get past something difficult, helped us learn and move through it more gracefully.

As I was experiencing growth and starting to feel better, I also felt more like a grownup. It was time for the next phase of healing in which I focused on becoming stronger and more stable. I had remembered and told my secrets, and it was time to focus on rebuilding and strengthening. It was time to THRIVE!

No More Breaking Down—
Now I'm Growing Strong

Thriving Phase of Recovery
(46 years old and beyond)

Although I struggled with this idea, at Patti's suggestion, a significant step in the beginning of my thriving phase was to write my story. I knew writing was therapeutic since my many years of journaling raw feelings were a tremendous help. She suggested I write about my experiences in the third person, which was a helpful tool; psychologically, it just seemed easier to describe what happened if I was someone else. She was right. I began my story with, "There was a little girl named Marie ..." and called it "The Unprotected Child."

The momentum of the thriving phase picked up as a result of telling my mother. It was good that more of my unconscious hidden beliefs were becoming conscious. I needed to become aware of the irrational self-hatred, so I could deal with it. My dark thoughts were moving from the deepest levels of hidden pain to conscious awareness.

One hidden belief that came to the surface was how much I hated my female sexual parts because they felt dirty and disgusting. I believed my body betrayed me, and I associated pain, panic, and devastation with parts of it. I felt my private parts were gross and I did not want to own them. That was because I associated them with being raped, and prior to this time, I had no idea I had these hidden beliefs.

Patti suggested I go to *The Vagina Monologues* play, which was being performed at the local college. My friend joined me, and it was a great experience. It helped me associate beauty and lightheartedness with vaginas. Who would have thought? It was a real breakthrough moment that took some time to fully sink in, and it felt like such a synchronistic event.

The play helped open a door for me. As a result, I thought about my private parts and rationalized how they were just as important as my hand or leg. I would think about how it wasn't my female parts' fault I was attacked, just like it wasn't my arm's fault. All of my parts are innocent. I listed the important roles each private part fulfills in life and realized over time they deserved to be loved and protected, just like the rest of me. As a result of this work, I felt more lightness and self-love.

How do you feel about having an inner dialogue with yourself? You could sit quietly and ask yourself how you feel about different parts of your body. You may be surprised, just as I was, at the answers that come back.

The person who wrote *The Vagina Monologues*, Eve Ensler, started a movement called V-Day to help end violence against women and girls. I hope there is a similar movement for our brother survivors, because they deserve to be protected and lifted up in a supportive spirit just like women do.

After the initial self-awareness concerning the misbeliefs about my body, I had let working on my body issues go for a while, and when it came up very clearly three years later, I addressed it again to heal more deeply. I knew it was time because I was synchronistically offered a free group class on mindful eating, my friend gave me a book called *A Course in Weight Loss* by Marianne Williamson, and I felt ready and open to love and connect with my body. I learned to trust that when the time is right, I'll know what and when to work on as God and my wise higher self guide me along.

I love Marianne's books! In her weight loss book, which I quote throughout my book, she trains you how to use your mind to love and integrate your body with the rest of yourself. It should be called a course in learning how to love yourself because when you do her book's writing exercises, you come out of it changed for the better: with self-love. I disconnected psychologically from my body as a child since I blamed it for being raped. Marianne explains that fat is symbolic of disowning some part of yourself. So, what I needed was to embrace my body and love it. I knew my extra weight was not about my eating; it was about how I felt about parts of myself, and it was time to heal my relationship with my body.

Several misbeliefs surfaced during this work, like secretly thinking fat was my armor protecting me and keeping me safe by looking less sexy. It's so important to get inside the mind and find those buried untruths.

> *"For many people, compulsive eating is tied to a fear of sex and of being sexy." "When I was beautiful, I was molested. Or, when I was beautiful, I was raped. Or, when I'm beautiful, I don't know how to handle the sexual attention."*
>
> —Marianne Williamson[30]

30

When you grasp excessively for anything in this world …
you deny what is trying to emerge from deep within you.
—Marianne Williamson[31]

I really had to work with myself, and then it became clear that the above quotes applied to me too. Years earlier, I would have told you the quote about the fear of being sexy did not hold true for me. Denial is so powerful, but when it's time to heal and you know the truth, denial doesn't have a chance.

* * *

Around the time of *The Vagina Monologues* play, I went to the Clothesline Project, which was also at the local college. There were many decorated shirts by domestic abuse survivors and their children symbolizing their journeys hanging on clotheslines outside over a grassy area, plus talks and other displays. I sat in on a talk on pornography Patti was giving. Wow, I don't think I was ready for that! I held it together, though, and watched because I felt I needed to know what was going on within the Internet world. This talk focused on how vulnerable women's bodies were being used inappropriately, but I'm sure there's plenty of this garbage about vulnerable men too.

I was in shock at what I saw and heard. It scared me to think of how my children could someday be exposed to such deranged and degrading material. For example, there are websites purporting women who want men to treat them like animals, then rape and purposely hurt them. There are other ridiculous ones like how women want their vaginal area stretched out so no other man would

31 Williamson, *A Course in Weight Loss*, 150.

want them. The bottom line with these dark pornographic sites is that women and men are just nonhuman sexual objects for others to use, abuse, and dispose of.

All of this is insinuating that the women, men, and children on these porn sites are objects without feelings, and that they don't have the same needs to be loved, respected, and protected as the people who want to hurt them. These people must be out of their minds! Our youth are exposed to this abusive and degrading material, and if they see it and read it enough, it starts to seep deep into their minds, especially at a young, impressionable age.

Pornography could easily entice the curious mind and act as a slow brainwashing agent, desensitizing people to awfully degrading images of children and adults. With so many lies being spewed out to justify the horrible treatment of these people on porn sites, combined with the money, drug use, and unconscious beliefs that draw people into acting out those degrading sexual roles, a disturbing stage is set for more violence. There is such an abundance of this mind-poisoning material that people could twist it into a validation that some people are whores and sex objects to be used and abused. This is the same dark, slippery slope that pedophiles engage in when trying to validate their own sick obsessions with children. They consume so many abusive images with children that over time, their minds justify their foul behavior. Porn addictions escalate like all addictions do over time. The highest tier of a porn addict or sex addict is rape and murder, and our prisons are full of porn addicts and sex addicts!

A whole culture of lies, degradation, torture, and misuse of women's, men's, and children's bodies for sexual pleasure is being played out on the Internet. This is not the typical porn that was around years ago as seen in the occasional Playboy magazine. There is so much of it, it's easily accessible, and it's really dark! Check out the following quote from an article about Pamela Anderson.

> *Multiple studies show that between 70 and 90 percent of female commercial sex workers—whether we're talking about nude models like Anderson, strippers, porn stars, or even prostitutes—were sexually abused as children.*
>
> —Kacie McCoy[32]

I'll bet a lot of male porn stars were victimized too, and I'll bet the estimates are low. Why do you think they're driven to that profession? If those porn stars were victims of abuse, they probably feel trapped in that world on some level in their minds and may be consciously unaware of it. Their boundaries and inner gauges for appropriate behavior are most likely broken or confused by their past abuse. The broken boundary system leads to confusion about attention, love, sex, power, and self-respect.

The following quote is taken from Dawn Eden's book *My Peace I Give You* about how her childhood sexual abuse drove her sexual behavior:

> *That was why I mentally dissociated myself from my victim identity in favor of a persona in which I could feel powerful. Since my greatest vulnerability was in the sexual realm, I chose to announce—through provocative dress, language, and behavior—that I was master of my own sexuality. Beneath the*

32 Kacie McCoy, "Sex may sell, but at what cost?" May 19, 2014, http://www.sheknows.com/love-and-sex/articles/1037807/pamela-anderson-reveals-childhood-sex-abuse,3/19/2004.

posturing, however, remained the soul of a little girl desperate to be told she was valued ***not*** *for what she did, but who she was.*

—Dawn Eden[33]

Amen to that!

Sexuality is complex. Many times, it's a dark part of the sexually abused survivor. I would like to share with you a prayer from Marianne Williamson's book *Illuminata* that addresses healing sexuality.

Dear God,
Please help me to heal the area of sex.
I feel so wounded, so damaged, betrayed by those
I thought were here to love me and protect me.
No words can say the pain I feel, when I
remember the abuse I suffered.
I surrender to You my memories and my anger
toward this person.
Please lift from me the burden of my resentment.
Please release me from this terrible pain.
Amen.[34]

I hope this prayer is helpful to you.

* * *

I grew increasingly aware of how my younger parts had become quieter since I told my mom about my trauma, and since my AS had been a successful protector of Little Marie. This set the stage for my AS to live my life more fully as an adult. I was feeling stronger and more confident about consciously interacting with the world as

33 Eden, *My Peace I Give You*, 54.

34 Williamson, *Illuminata*, 176.

my mature self. The possibility that I could be normal was peeking through the door, and I was so grateful for this progress.

Looking nice and losing weight was starting to feel okay. I would occasionally have flashes of shuddering fear, like the day I saw a lovely and shapely woman walking down the street in a short-fitted dress. When I saw her, I tensed up and felt afraid for her. I caught myself and said, "She is a strong, beautiful woman who has the right to dress as she pleases and express herself. She won't be raped because of her looks. It's okay for others to admire her—it doesn't mean they will attack her. Relax. She and I are safe and okay." I reminded myself that in reality, rape statistics show that looks, shape, and clothes have nothing to do with whether someone is raped or not. Rape is much more about the victim's vulnerability in the presence of someone predisposed to perpetration.

Another thing that would create a shuddering fear was when someone would come to my door unannounced. I would panic and refuse to answer. I didn't like leaving the front door open because it made me feel vulnerable, and I wanted to choose whether I was going to let someone in or not. The memory of my second rape, when I opened the front door to an unexpected person who attacked me, drove that fear.

There was this sweet young lady who babysat my children, and she would periodically just show up at my door. Panic would hit, and I would run to the room that had a window to the driveway, trying to peek out and see who it was. When I saw it was her, I would calm down. After a few of her surprise visits, I had a sense that this young woman was unknowingly being of help to me. I was learning that not every unexpected person at my door was going to attack. I practiced noting consciously what was happening so that I could learn to defuse my panic response. Over time, I would open the door to her beautiful, safe face and realize it was okay, I was healing a bit more each time. One day, she came by when the front door was already open, and I thought I was going to have a heart attack. Fight-or-flight was in full swing with my heart racing and my breathing quick and shallow, as I flew into the office to check the driveway and then shakily approached the door, where I saw it was her. Phew! What a relief.

Everything I needed came when the time was right. I'm taking notice of that truth and working to internalize that message! I'm striving to remember that it's okay to trust and have faith in my healing. I still get twinges of anxiety with the whole front door thing, but it has greatly improved. What I was working on with the front door is called *exposure therapy*. It's when you slowly expose yourself to an anxiety-provoking situation and see that you are okay. Slow exposure to a panic trigger will lessen the panic or fear over time, and this has worked well for me. However, too much exposure too soon only makes the situation worse.

The above unexpected visitor example was one of many that demonstrated how my triggered panic—which were involuntary physical and emotional reactions—were moving from the primitive survival part of my brain (amygdala) to the conscious, more voluntary and rational cerebral cortex, where I could work with it. This work gave me the opportunity to choose *not* to ask our babysitter to stop her surprise visits so that I could purposely work on my panic response and shift it to a more rational, relaxed place. I didn't tell her about it until after the fact.

Prior to reaching this point on my healing path, I would have gotten angry and told her to let me know in advance when she was coming over. I would have refused to answer the door. However, now I was using her visits as an opportunity to heal and grow, but with limits. I did make a deal with myself that if I got too freaked out or felt I couldn't deal with it, I would ask her to call first. I refused to continually put myself through too much because it was my job to hold my boundaries and to be kind to myself.

Another area of progress I noticed happened one day on a call with my spiritual health coach (SHC). I would sometimes go into a terror-shaking state, and she would have different tools (see Appendix B, Self-Empowerment Coping Tools) to guide me through it with strength. Every time, she helped me see that I was strong and could work with techniques to move myself out of terror. Just because panic was triggered didn't mean I had to go down. It was important to have her there with me, guiding me and giving me confidence to persevere as I practiced using these various techniques. That's why I recommend doing this kind of coping skills training with a professional therapist or other professional healing modality you gravitate toward.

On the day of the call, I was losing it in a panic attack, and I used one of her simple tools, which was to laugh like a lunatic as she laughed with me for several minutes. It knocked my mind off the scared track, and I was able to regain my composure. I was amazed by this. How simple is that? Oh, and I love this one. I would picture myself as bigger than Earth, and picture the problem or fear as a mere speck that I would pick up, crush in my hands, and flick out into the universe. My SHC used so many techniques; it was awesome working with her. I believe she helped heal me on spiritual, psychological, and physical levels by teaching me practical and easy-to-use coping skills to add to my toolbox. Mostly, though, it was her loving, centered presence that was the most healing aspect of our work together. She was an empowering witness.

Note: With my work in 2015–1016, I learned to embrace fear when it emerged and love and parent it with acceptance like I did with my younger parts. It's very effective! It's a new mind-set: working on my inner self instead of focusing on the external world to distract myself from uncomfortable feelings.

I continued to deal with anxiety on and off but continued to practice my new coping skills. I'm grateful to be aware of how anxiety works in me because I didn't in the past, and now I can observe it and work with it. In the past, it would secretly haunt me, and I wanted to self-medicate. Now, I know what's bothering me, and I can use my self-soothing tools instead of self-destructive behaviors to get through it. Not perfectly, though, because I don't think that exists. When I do occasionally revisit a self-destructive coping skill, it doesn't last long, and it's less intense. Then I forgive myself and remind myself that I'm trying my best, and that's good enough.

Over time I had slowly pulled the veil off my hidden mind and exposed the darkness that lay within. Living with less fear is a practice that takes a lot of time, but it pays off in a big way. My fear is just a thought my mind makes up, and I'm trying not to buy into it. I have confidence, peace, and a strong spiritual connection—these guide me and prop me up so that I can show up for life. My SHC helped me see that as I healed myself, I lifted my family up too by being a stronger base for them as well. Good stuff!

* * *

At one point, I was doing a different kind of visual healing work with my SHC, both while I was in session and on my own. I could see my body getting energetically cleaned out with openings at my hands, feet, the top of my head, etc., and a lot of black gooey stuff coming out. After it drained, I would then visualize water rinsing through me, and finally I would fill myself up with white crystals and bright light, as Angela taught me to do. Sometimes these visual energetic cleansing sessions led to forgiveness work, as noted in the journal entries below:

> *One day, after completing my morning prayers and affirming that I'm bigger than any problem or sickness, I looked into my baby self's eyes and began some inner child work. I kept repeating, "I love you, I love you so much." Then I said, "I forgive you, I forgive you for everything," over and over. I did the same thing with my toddler self. Next, as I was telling my ADS I love you, she bent down and started vomiting piles and piles of a disgusting, gloppy substance. I asked my ADS for permission before I did anything because she knew what she needed, and I wanted her to have control over what was happening to her body. A large black mass was trying to come out of her mouth, and she motioned for me to take it out. I couldn't do it alone, so I called Archangel Michael and my guardian angels to help.*
>
> *Next, I saw all these energetic threads coming from my ADS's body. I asked her if she wanted me to pull each one. She said yes, and I gently pulled them out. The first ones were attached to her throat*

(first rape) and at the end of the first group was a seed. I handed it to Archangel Michael. Then I was pulling them from my private areas, stomach, and lungs. When we were done working on my ADS's body, it looked saggy and deflated, so I filled her up with gold-and-silver light and talked to my ADS about how much I love her and how she is forgiven. I said, "I am filled with my God Source's Light. I have everything I need. I am whole. I stand in my light, and I am full of wholeness. I am FREE!"

The next day, I checked in with my younger selves, and they were all quietly nestled within my AS, and my ADS was healing. I felt so moved by this experience, and then I wrote Witness. It's one of my favorite poems because it encapsulates my recovery process, and one of the many gifts of forgiveness.

* * *

WITNESS

In the darkness, I survived for forty-six years.
My victim place wrapped its hands
Around my neck and squeezed my light out.
My inner torment and unending well of pain and loneliness.

My pieces of self, so many escaped, ran in terror.
Scattered and shattered from the well of trauma.
Finally, I knew the truth and sat with terror,
Rage, and such grief.
But at the core, hidden,
Was self-hatred shrouded in shame.
And once released,
Then, and only then, was there room
For self-love and self-forgiveness.

I did not know this was a key.
I called my pieces of self back home
To my crater where I belong.
My cylinder of light filled with diamond crystals.
My red cord of life, connecting me, rooting me, from the
Heavens to the center of the Earth.
I watched my pieces come home, and all my beautiful mother
Containers (helpers) helped distribute and balance me.

I feel joy and love and peace and gratitude.
I thought this could not be.

A Witness—I am a witness to my own wholeness.
Approaching my summit where I can be confident and wise.
Own the light that is me, and share a message of Truth,
Spiritual Connection, and Hope.

A message to those who may be spiritually seeking,
seeking Truth, or those, who may be in this moment,
Ready to give up and die in darkness.

Never Never Never Give Up.
My dear sister and brother,
There really is hope.
Let others hold hope for you till you can.
Just don't give up.

Seek and Wait
For your personal miracle of healing.
Wait till you can be a witness to your wholeness.
Wait till you can live in your light,
And experience a peace you may have
Thought you would never know.

* * *

Around this time, my SAC got promoted, and we had our last therapy session through the sexual assault services program. Thank you, Patti! Her timing to end our therapy was excellent, and I was happy for her. I was ready to continue healing with others in my support circle and very grateful that our sessions didn't have to end before I was ready. I was, and will always be, grateful to Patti for her loving and knowledgeable midwifing me through so much pain and confusion. How can I ever thank her for saving my life? That's what her help felt like.

A few weeks later, I did some forgiveness work from when I was a new mom with my first child, to deal with the guilt I had over my periods of instability when my son was very young. See how the healing work/forgiveness is moving forward in time from childhood to adulthood? Next, I asked my younger AS if she would like to rest with Jesus by calm waters or go in our corral. She said, "I want you (my current AS) because you feel good, and I want to join with my younger selves."

Wow, I wasn't expecting that. It made me feel happy and whole, and I recognized that this was another step forward in self-integration. It was an empowering experience to practice forgiveness. A few days after I did this forgiveness work, I worked on forgiving myself for everything and telling myself how deeply I loved myself. I also worked on releasing my fears about being self-confident and standing in my light. *I could feel myself healing.* Recovery is possible, and I'm so grateful. I don't see a defined end to my healing work. It's more like a lifelong voyage with required weekly management, while reaping the benefits of the work thus far.

A month or so after doing my young mother forgiveness work, a new phase of my healing was blossoming. I was learning to have faith in myself and deal with my fear of self-confidence. Being confident in who I am and what I can offer others was a whole new experience. I liked it, but I was a clumsy beginner who needed more maturing. Can you relate to lacking self-confidence? Isn't it so limiting? The following is an entry from my journal, and I hope you can embrace the parts you identify with.

I'm saying this out loud because I need to hear it. Nothing is going to keep me down! NOTHING! My life wasn't saved by Divine intervention just so I could lie in my bed full of fear. I lived through multiple life-threatening rapes and didn't kill myself from self-blame, shame, and hatred. It's a miracle I'm alive. I have a passion—a story to share—a burning desire to reach out to those who are tormented and traumatized, and to be a guide or pillar of hope that each and every person, no matter what they are suffering, can hold hope for healing.

I will not allow fear to hold me down any longer. Fear is a lie in me—a dream that my fear mind dreams. It's not truth. I make it up and hold myself captive with it. NO MORE! No more standing in my light and owning my power and then self-sabotaging with foreboding fear that rises up within me. NO MORE! I am confident, and I'm moving forward. Fear is a thought, and it has no power over me! I know who I am, and I know what I want to do. It has taken many years of work to have this knowing. Like I'm going to let some lie or made-up irrational fear hold me back? HELL NO!

Every time my imagined fear comes up in any form (physical or negative thinking) like, "See, you can't do anything, you're broken," I address it. "That's a lie, I know I'm a spiritual being full of peace and love, and I'm confident in me and my story, and I'm moving forward and leaving fear in the dust." I say this with power and confidence, and I will keep saying it until I undo my mind's dream of fear. I forgive myself for believing in the fear, and I let it go. After all, my fear is just a mistaken perception.

Wow! I'm really seeing growth at this point. I never would have dreamed this was possible before or during my crisis phase

***

I believe the greatest gift I can give to my family, the world, and myself is forgiveness. It creates a peaceful mind by setting a person free, instead of keeping them down in judgment. Forgiveness is love. I'm on a spiritual road of letting my fear mind go and embracing the Divine within myself and others.

I wouldn't have expected myself to do deep spiritual forgiveness work before or during my crisis phase because I needed to get some stuff out first. If my hands are full of fear, anger, and weakness, where is the room for love, forgiveness, and strength? When it was time, I naturally gravitated to deeper forgiveness work, and I believe you will too. I intuitively knew I needed to do this, and I didn't care if others thought it was necessary. When I was ready, teachers showed up and helped me move forward.

You can't reach for anything new if your hands are still full of yesterday's junk.

—Louise Smith[35]

Please take this in. Do you struggle with forgiveness? If you

35 "Louise Smith Quotes," accessed January 18, 2018, http://www.quoteswave.com/picture-quotes/105761.

do, try to let it go for now. If you feel guilt for not wanting to or not feeling ready to forgive, try to let that go too. The struggle, lack of willingness, or resistance is your inner self letting you know it isn't time yet. There are other things you need to do first on your healing journey to make room for forgiveness. However long it takes is okay, and if there's someone pushing you or making you feel guilty about not forgiving, you may need space from them or boundaries put in place. Another person will often push you because of some of their own unconscious unfinished business, and it really isn't about you. So, it's okay to go at *your* pace.

You and only you decide when you are ready to move forward on your healing journey. There's no question in my mind that if you patiently tune into your wise higher self and ask what is next, you will be guided. Trust; try to trust in yourself. See what you are naturally attracted to, who is in your life, what books/movies/music you gravitate toward. A good therapist can be instrumental in helping you see your own inner wisdom. So, please, trust the wise healer in you because I believe with all my being that no one knows you like you do when it comes to your journey. And your journey will be different from another person's journey; it will be unique to you with your strengths, weaknesses, and gifts.

As I progressed through my spiritual healing journey, I had more periods of peace and would visit my pain less frequently and with less intensity. I could meet my pain from a stronger foundation. There were moments when the reality of what I had been through slowly sunk deeper into my awareness. I could take it in more without dissociating. The following journal entry is one example of this.

As I come out of my torment—each step I take up my ladder of hope, love, and healing—I'm amazed by the strength of the human spirit, at what survivors are capable of enduring while still going on with life. I realize how strong we all are. The healing work is all worth it to arrive here in this place and be in a state of peace.

I need to hear about empowerment, and I believe other survivors need to hear it too. It's a message that's difficult to internalize for someone who comes from prolonged childhood trauma. Each and every survivor has incredible strength within them. We have more than we could have imagined, and it's reinforcing for us to acknowledge our strength and how far we've come.

Note: Please take this in. You have the strength to endure whatever it is you need to live through in order for you to heal. Throughout your personal journey, please remember that you're never alone with your pain. We stand in solidarity as survivors and spiritual brothers and sisters. On a spiritual level, I see us as one spiritual child of God with the same powerful inner strength. Please go ahead and take that next step up your ladder of healing.

* * *

At forty-six years old, I had a car accident that triggered my old trauma and showed me how my healing work had set up a foundation that carried me through a very hard experience. I wrote an account of the accident later that day in my journal.

I just had a car accident while driving my children to school. As I went to cross an intersection, BAM! That was a first in thirty years of driving! I'm scared and shaky as I move around in what feels like a dream. I'm checking on my children and helping my daughter calm down and then I walk around the other driver's car and sense intense emotion. I notice she has a handwritten sign in her back window that reads, "ALL MEN ARE CREEPS—signed 'ME'." Chills run down my spine. I'm approaching her now. I see her baby in the back in his car seat crying, but he looks okay. The driver is young and hysterical, and she has tattoos and piercings. She cries out at me, "Why did you do that to me? Why?"

I know she's a victim of more than this car crash; I just know she's a trauma survivor. I recognize it in her, and she appears to be overreacting to the situation. Don't get me wrong, a car accident involving children where both cars get totaled is scary, but it's as if she's reacting to something else, something more. She's completely oblivious to her baby, which I find difficult to cope with. My old trauma is rising up, and I'm triggered on multiple levels, and I feel I'm going to collapse as the ground feels like it's sinking beneath my feet and despair flirts with me. I use a grounding tool by firmly repeating in my mind my name and my age and that "I'm an adult, I'm safe, and I'll stay in the present. I will not fall into that hole!" Grounding stabilizes me, and I start praying for the woman and her baby by asking the angels to wrap their wings around them and comfort them. Meanwhile, there are two women who stopped when they saw the accident and are calling for help to assist us. God bless them, they are a godsend.

I know that if that woman driving the other car is a trauma survivor, then any past trauma is likely at the surface and she's in fact coping with more than the accident we just had. Taking into consideration the sign on her window, it's making sense to me. The emergency response personnel are great with my children and me, but unfortunately, I'm hearing them judging the other driver's reactions as being way over the top. They just don't understand.

We are all at the hospital now, and I just learned my kids are fine, thank God. Some hospital staff are complaining about the other driver's supposed overreaction and drama. I pray for her some more. Soon after we arrive, a dear friend of mine comes to the hospital, and her presence is comforting. At one point, I see someone holding the other driver's baby, who looks fine. The baby looks at me with a great big baby smile, and I know he's okay as I cry tears of relief.

I'm reflecting on the day's events and thinking about my children and how strong they are. They took each piece of the accident in stride, even though I know they were scared. We went through it together, supporting each other. I'm also grateful that as I thought about coming very close to falling in my trauma hole of despair that seemed to call out to me, I held my ground and said no to that fear-victim dream. Instead, I chose to use my tools and empower myself to move through the whole process one moment and one step at a time. As I further reflected on looking in the window at that terrified woman and seeing the note in her back window, it felt like I was looking in a mirror at the old me. The experience was intense, and I learned many lessons, some of which were that I was no longer a victim, I was strong, and could handle anything with God's help. I had started that day with a car accident and tremendous guilt, but ended it with forgiveness for all involved.

As I witnessed myself getting stronger, I was able to take in my traumas at a deeper level of understanding. During my forty-sixth year, about two years after remembering the rape in my home, I had a visual experience that helped me take in the rape event at a much deeper level. This visual experience acted as an awareness tool, and it was not a memory.

> **(SHIELDS UP)** I was driving home, and for the first time, I took in deeply the magnitude of how close I came to death all those years ago. I saw an image in my mind of my young body lying lifeless on those stairs with my throat cut and blood all around me. Then I realized how my mother almost came home to find her little girl murdered. Prior to this memory, I could only tell the events with limited feeling in a somewhat detached state. But on this day, I fully took in what had happened and how many people's lives would have changed if God hadn't intervened. I also took in how grateful I was that my life was spared. **(DEEP BREATH)**

The mind is amazing in the way that it lets more and more come into awareness at deeper and deeper levels slowly over time. Many trauma survivors don't fully take in the enormity of what we lived through due to our mind's defense mechanisms. Awareness comes when and if we are ready, and only if it's needed for the survivor's healing and ability to move forward.

Isn't it interesting that this deep realization came while I was doing forgiveness work with myself and connecting with God? Deeper awareness typically occurred at those moments. I don't think the healing I experienced from forgiveness would have had such permanent results if I hadn't allowed God to work through me. Where there is genuine love and forgiveness, there is healing—permanent healing.

After I saw the gruesome image of my child self on the stairs, I continued to work on forgiving my mother for not being home, on myself for opening the door, and on forgiving the rapist who had so much hate. I believe he hated himself, and I think he projected his hate onto me in a sick, compulsive, and unsuccessful attempt to relieve his own torment. But his actions only fed a seemingly endless loop of fear, hatred, and suffering. As he killed off parts of me, I believe he also killed off parts of himself. That's why many pedophiles' eyes look soulless to me. I know they suffer too, and their cruel acts come from devastation within them.

Forgiving the rapist had *nothing* to do with saying what he did was okay. It was about releasing the death grip of the rape; I thought it was his grip on me, but I finally realized I was allowing the event to hold me prisoner. I gave up my power for a while, believing he had a hold on me. I held onto my rage toward him, as it was my right to be angry, but unfortunately, my rage just kept holding me hostage. I had to be the one to let go. My healing is an inside job, and I'm responsible for my perceptions and reactions.

To forgive is to set a prisoner FREE and discover that the prisoner was YOU.

—Lewis B. Smedes[36]

It was scary to experience the deeper awareness of that rape, but also healing. I needed to know the truth. Each awareness or bit of truth allowed me to release more, which led to more freedom and peace. There's no doubt about it: If we want our healing work to last, fear must be walked *through*, not around. And we certainly can't avoid it.

36 "Lewis B. Smedes Quotes," BrainyQuote, accessed January 18, 2018, https://www.brainyquote.com/quotes/lewis_b_smedes_135524.

As far as forgiving myself and my mother, even though my AS knows that my mother and I did nothing wrong, I needed to do this work with my CS because this is how that part of me saw it. My CS blamed herself, and my negating that from an adult perspective just kept her stuck. I accepted that she blamed herself, and I forgave her over and over by doing ICW. "I love you and forgive you for everything, Little Marie. I love you so much. I forgive you. I forgive all of it. I forgive you, Marie for everything. My love for you is without conditions or exceptions." As I watched her cry her little heart out while my AS held her in my mind's eye, I knew she was releasing and moving toward peace. Oh, how I've yearned for my younger parts to feel loved, whole, and peaceful.

After first sitting with her while she released her pain, I continued to hold Little Marie as I sensed an opening for me to tell her what I believe happened from my adult perspective. My brother and sister survivors, this is for your child self too:

> *"It was no one's fault but the person who chose to hurt you. You were supposed to be loved, guided, and taken care of by the adults in your life. It was the adults' responsibility to protect you and make sure you were safe. Children automatically think it's their fault—all children, not just you. Telling yourself it was your fault isn't true. In fact, it's an outright lie."*
>
> *Her eyes got big, and she said "Really?"*
>
> *I continued, "I'm so terribly sorry your little heart was broken, that you went through childhood with so much anxiety and carried a heavy burden of feeling responsible to watch out for yourself. I'm so sorry you had a core belief that you can't trust people, you can't trust yourself, and that people hurt you at any moment. I'm so, so*

> *sorry your childhood was stolen. I know those feelings are scary and painful for you."*
>
> *My child self nodded and cried. We sobbed together and grieved the loss of my childhood in the context of trauma.*

It took a long time to reach this level of healing. I first needed to release a lot of rage, fear, grief, and that damn shame that acted like a hidden disease, slowly killing me off from deep within. The rapists murdered parts of me, and my guilt and shame took out even more. But as I forgave myself, I began to heal past the guilt and shame. I extended my forgiveness to others, and in this way, obtained my freedom and peace. The self-forgiveness wasn't about my trauma being my fault. Instead, it was connected to my CS's false belief that it was her fault. The most beautiful result of forgiveness, which is a form of self-love, is how much more capable I am now to love God, my family, and others. *Forgiveness with God's help is the most critical part of my healing journey.*

Your relationship with yourself is the source that all other relationships are mirrored from. If that source is judgmental and critical, then you will be that way with others, and that is what you will perceive from others. The more deeply you accept and love yourself, the more capacity you will have to love others and receive love back, and the clearer your connection with God will become. Those are beautiful gifts!

* * *

At almost forty-seven, my trauma healing work is quieting down. My spiritual growth work has taken the front seat, and I'm still working with my SHC on a regular basis. One day I was meditating and saw the rapists vaguely in my mind's eye. I went to one of them to do forgiveness work and realized my preschool self was at my side. I asked her if she was sure she wanted to forgive him, and she nodded yes. We stood side by side, holding hands, and forgave together. It was healing and empowering, and we cried a lot. Then my adolescent and teen selves forgave. At the end, we all put our hatred and fear on God's altar with complete trust and faith that God would take care of it. I felt calm and hopeful. It was wonderful to see my younger self forgiving instead of attacking.

We forgave by feeling love in our hearts and extending it out to the rapists while we spoke to them: "We forgive you and are sorry you are tormented. We pray for love and peace in your heart. God bless you with healing."

The emotional lows were showing up less frequently now, and were manageable. They were short lived, and I wasn't going as low as I used to. I was even stringing lots of peaceful days together, and wasn't taking any medication for depression, ADD—nothing! I was holding my own. Yes! Only a year earlier, I had resigned myself to thinking I would be on psychiatric drugs for the rest of my life. I'm open to taking them in the future if need be. But for now, I'm grateful I don't need to. I was also able to have some wine just to enjoy it. I didn't need to use it in excess as medicine to numb my pain anymore.

As I read over my twenty years of journals, I'm noticing phases of healing. The phases were not linear, as seeing one phase ending and the next one starting, but rather, new ones would periodically appear, and the old ones would reappear as needed. You know the peeling of the onion metaphor, where you peel away and explore deeper and deeper layers of yourself? It wasn't just layer after layer but many aspects and angles of each layer too.

To summarize, my healing phases began with identifying my feelings and connecting with myself, or *finding a sense of self.* Then I went on to psychologically *separating from my fused family of origin* and doing codependency work and then to *inner child* and *shadow work*. Next, the phases went into growing *spiritually and creatively* and then *learning healthier life skills*. The phases continued into *remembering my trauma* and letting all the stuffed emotion out, then went into *telling my secrets*, and finally to *forgiveness and peace*. I believe all healing roads lead to forgiveness and peace. Once you meet up with forgiveness and peace, it doesn't mean you're done. You can still revisit other phases, but with a stronger foundation, spiritual strength, and resolve, because you have gotten a taste of the most beautiful gift—a peaceful heart.

I also don't deal with anger to the same degree I used to, and I can even see some value in it. Anger has a place—it can tell me when boundaries are being crossed, or it can act like a blanket over sadness or as necessary fuel for courage to speak up. I realized that anger is an important red flag and a tool that gets my attention. I try to take notice when I'm feeling angry and ask myself, "What line is being crossed?" or "What is going on under the anger?" Once I'm not a puppet to my anger, other deeper feelings can come into awareness. This new clarity is an important guide for what I need to do next, which is usually setting a boundary or doing some forgiveness work. So anger isn't something to avoid—it's a warning flag to get our attention to go within and work with ourselves.

* * *

I decided a next step for my healing was to go see a shaman my friend highly recommended. While he was working on me, it was interesting how he zeroed in on healing my root chakra. That is the energetic area that addresses feeling safe and trusting versus mistrusting, and it's associated with one's sexual self. He was drumming and singing over me, and I sensed a tingling feeling. A few days after seeing the shaman, I saw a part of myself in my mind's eye, like I did with my younger selves. Whatever part she was, she looked sickly—very anorexic and scared. I asked my teen self who it was, and she said it was my sexual self.

When I tried to reach out to her, she vanished. She is shunned and invisible, and she represents pain. I felt awful that I didn't know about her. I'm connected with my younger, spiritual, emotional, physical, and intellectual selves, but what about my sexual self? This is a foggy area for me. I realized this to be the next branch on my healing tree to be embraced, surrendered to, and loved.

Once I started interacting with this new part of me, I asked her name, and she it is Lotus. She appeared to embody the concept of abandonment. That name seemed so appropriate after all the lotus references during my healing journey. My younger selves and I rallied around and talked to her about how we started out vulnerable and scared, but she could grow strong just like we did, and that we are still healing. She looked overwhelmed but intrigued.

She then appeared to regress to infancy, so I invited her to hop in my sling and safely snuggle while I carried her. It was comforting to look into her eyes with adoring love because I knew this was healing since I was offering my heart. My younger selves and I kept repeating, *"WE SEE YOU, YOU ARE PART OF US, WE LOVE YOU AND WELCOME*

YOU TO BE LOVED AND ACCEPTED EXACTLY AS YOU ARE." We all cried and offered to let her into our safe house or take her to one of Jesus's wounds. She chose Jesus.

Is sexuality a difficult experience for you? You can gently embrace wherever you're at and take baby steps to connect with your sexual self, but you may need some professional help with this. Sexual abuse creates so many blocks with the survivor's sexual belief system and expression. It creates involuntary physical responses—like avoidance or disgust when it doesn't make sense to have that reaction.

As of writing this, Lotus has been slowly growing older and looking more alive. What a beautiful gift healing work is. Thank you, Lotus, and my younger selves, and all my other parts (spiritual, emotional, creative, intellectual, and physical). I love myself, and my prayer for all you survivors is to love every part of yourself without condition.

Note: Please take this in. I implore you to do your healing work. Slow or fast, start and stop and start again, just go at your own pace—as long as you keep going. You deserve to heal. Please don't give up. Your healing, your gift of peace, is unimaginably beautiful, and you deserve it. I want you to know your torment is real and valid, and so is your potential to heal. Your peace is waiting for you.

* * *

Throughout my journey, I have always needed a caring professional or group to reach out to when I needed extra support. At times it was a therapist, herbalist, chiropractor, psychic, hypnotherapist, spiritual healer, women's group, or AA or OA meeting. Even if you're not sure you were abused, try to zero in on someone who specializes in what you suspect may have happened to you. I found that I needed a safe person to stand with me and be a witness. *I needed someone to remind me that I'm strong, that this will pass, and not to give up before my miracle of healing happens.* What a powerfully healing dynamic a loving witness is! I don't believe that I or anyone else is supposed to do deep healing from trauma alone. Each of us is so intricately connected, so how could we be expected to do this scary work alone and still be able to function, or just survive it? One alternative chiropractor told me I was in a process of learning to love myself and he wanted me to picture myself as a box with a bow around it and see how I was a gift to the world. Thank you, Dr. Bump.

Would you try imagining yourself as a beautifully wrapped gift to the world and yourself with all your unique strengths? Go ahead and gift yourself with that vision of truth.

I so appreciate every person who has guided me on my healing journey. Others can now see my gifts and enjoy the individual I am. It took so long for me to be able to see and love myself and to enjoy the gift of loving myself.

> *If you keep focusing on your flaws, listening to what other people are saying, you can miss your destiny. Instead, remind yourself that you are valuable, you are equipped, you are anointed, you are approved.*
>
> —Joel Osteen[37]

My different therapists modeled how I should treat myself by how they treated and guided me over the years. Their guidance led me

37 "Do Not Focus on Your Flaws," *Positive Outlooks* (blog), January 17, 2014, https://positiveoutlooksblog.com/2014/01/17/do-not-focus/.

to learning how to listen to my inner wisdom, and that is a gift I'm praying we all acquire.

* * *

I'm chomping at the bit to share this with you! As of writing this paragraph, I AM CELEBRATING that I'm emotionally balanced and able to function! I'm not having the intense visions, and I can't remember the last time I had a nightmare. My journal entries and poems are full of spiritual inspiration and hope. I'm literally a different person. I attribute this to the many years of healing work you've read about in my story. Are you ready for this: I can't remember the last time I had an intense mood disturbance that seemed to come out of nowhere from my past. Can you believe it? It has been so long that I can't remember. I was plagued with devastating moods coming out of nowhere for many years. I'm crying tears of relief as I'm writing this to you. I feel free from my trauma torment. I'm going to say it again: *I feel free from my trauma torment!* I still experience some discomfort from my traumas from time to time, but nothing like the devouring torment I used to feel. It's manageable now.

I'm grateful to know where my pain came from, to have felt it, and then to have released it. My pain also allows me to empathize deeply with others. Best of all, I'm not afraid of my pain. I'm no longer afraid of myself and what I might find.

As all people do, I experience difficult times in life, but I have my coping toolbox of self-love available when they arise. I am occasionally triggered. At those times, I turn to my toolbox and those in my support network, for whom I am very grateful.

Epilogue

Paying It Forward

(Ongoing)

I want to share with you the next phase I'm looking forward to in my recovery. I've mentioned how I struggled with whether I would ever be well enough to work outside the home again. Many survivors choose to reach out to other survivors in some capacity, as an expression of wanting to help another who knows how hard it is to heal from childhood trauma. I too am working toward this goal, I'm making it my career path. In addition, even though I've been working on my healing, all along I've been doing informal social work and studying clinical social work, with special attention to learning how to help others heal from trauma.

I'm a psychotherapist at heart, and specializing in trauma recovery is definitely my focus. There are trauma re-processing healing modalities available that are advancing the understanding of how to assist a survivor with trauma to heal more quickly and effectively. Some of these modalities are EMDR, Brainspotting, Somatic Experiencing, and ICW, among other subspecialties like Mindfulness, which can all be used in a psychotherapeutic environment. I started my certified trauma therapist (CTT) extensive training with Judy Crane, a leading trauma recovery expert, and I'm amazed at what I'm learning! It'll take some time to accomplish this training, but I'm beyond excited about being able to effectively help others. Taking ten to twenty years to find healing is much too long! I recommend Judy Crane's trauma healing facility, The Guest House Ocala, if you're looking for a place to heal with a supportive team of trauma experts.

Since I was a stay-at-home mom for a while, it feels empowering to get back into the workforce. However, even though I'm anxious about it, I'm also excited about working in a field I feel passionate about. Down the road, I would also like to host workshops and speak to groups of survivors. But I need to remind myself to take it slow and easy.

As part of preparing to be a helpful guide and witness for others, I like to alternate reading survivor memoirs and professional research books. Participating in online forums is helping me continue to heal and teaching me so much about myself and others. My favorite forum is isurvive.org. What an amazing anonymous place to share all aspects of recovery with such loving, supportive survivors who totally understand what you're talking about. The powerful strength of this group of people standing by each other's side through brutal pain and challenges is truly inspiring, and yet saddening. To hold hope for, and sit with, others as they forge forward with their healing work warms my heart. Saying I'm grateful doesn't even touch how thankful I am to sit with brother or sister survivors while they heal.

Well, guess what? I'm celebrating this phase of healing, and I've been back at work for some time! Yes, I did it! I love being back at work as a therapist, to feel all I've been through has been in preparation for this phase, in which I can act as a loving witness to my clients in my office, which is an open lotus flower for their healing.

Now I see my own lotus flower with ALL my petals stretched out—thriving and growing stronger!

Dear Brother and Sister Survivors,

Thank you for being a witness to my awakening to healing. Don't forget to look through the helpful information in the Appendix sections. I pray for your healing, for you to be supported, and for you to find what and who you need to help you heal. May you be blessed with peace and joy. May you realize your wholeness. And may your dreams come true.

Love,

Marie

If the finish line feels too far away, don't look at it, just look down at your feet and take your next best step.
—Dr. Melissa McCreery[38]

38 Dr. Melissa McCreery, Too Much on Her Plate, http://toomuchonherplate.com/stop-stress-eating-motivation-quotes/.

Thank You

You can sign up on my website to be notified of any pending book releases or updated content, plus, receive a free guided meditation for relaxation. By subscribing you will be first in line for exclusive deals and future book giveaways.

I'm looking forward to hearing from you!

To Sign up now: www.witnessawakening.com/witnessawakeningbook

Thank you for reading, and thank you so much for choosing to be on this journey with me.

Please do not hesitate to connect with me if you have any questions come up about this book, or if you just want someone to chat with.

I would be happy to hear from you and I enjoy connecting with readers.

In Gratitude,

–Marie McCarthy

A Quick Favor Please?

Before you go can I ask you for a quick favor?

Would you please leave this book a review on Amazon?

Your review is very important, as it can help this book to reach more trauma survivors.

Please take a quick minute to go to Amazon and leave this book an honest review. I promise it doesn't take very long, and it can help this book get into the hands of someone else whom it may help.

Thank You,

–Marie McCarthy

Bibliography

"Anaïs Nin Quotes." Goodreads. Accessed January 11, 2018. https://www.goodreads.com/quotes/2846-and-the-day-came-when-the-risk-to-remain-tight.

Barker, Robert L. *Social Work Dictionary*. 5th ed. NASW Press, 2003.

Bass, Ellen, and Lauren Davis. *The Courage to Heal: A Guide for Women Survivors of Childhood Sexual Abuse*. 4th ed. New York: Harper Collins, 1994.

"Carl Jung Quotes." BrainyQuote. Accessed January 16, 2018. https://www.brainyquote.com/quotes/carl_jung_101266.

"Child Sexual Abuse Statistics." Darkness to Light. Accessed November 28, 2017. http://www.d2l.org/the-issue/statistics.

Chopra, Deepak, and Oprah Winfrey. *21-Day Meditation Challenge, Miraculous Relationships*. 6 CD Set. Chopra Center, 2013.

"Do Not Focus on Your Flaws." *Positive Outlooks* (blog). January 17, 2014. https://positiveoutlooksblog.com/2014/01/17/do-not-focus/.

Eden, Dawn. *My Peace I Give You*. Notre Dame: Ave Maria Press, 2012.

Grohol, John. "Post-Traumatic Stress Disorder, Introduction to PTSD Symptoms & Treatment." Psych Central. https://psychcentral.com/disorders/ptsd/.

Grohol, John. "15 Common Defense Mechanisms." Psych Central. https://psychcentral.com/lib/15-common-defense-mechanisms/.

"Lewis B. Smedes Quotes." BrainyQuote. Accessed January 18, 2018. https://www.brainyquote.com/quotes/lewis_b_smedes_135524.

"Louise Smith Quotes." Accessed January 18, 2018. http://www.quoteswave.com/picture-quotes/105761.

Lupton, Rosamund. *Sister: A Novel.* New York: Crown, 2011.

Mallette, Patti, with A. J. Gregory. *Nowhere But Up: The Story of Justin Bieber's Mom*. Grand Rapids: Revell, 2012.

"Marvin J. Ashton Quotes." Goodreads. Accessed January 10, 2018. https://www.goodreads.com/quotes/51853-if-we-could-look-into-each-other-s-hearts-and-understand.

McCoy, Kacie. "Sex may sell, but at what cost?" May 19, 2014. http://www.sheknows.com/love-and-sex/articles/1037807/pamela-anderson-reveals-childhood-sex-abuse,3/19/2004.

McCreery, Melissa. Too Much on Her Plate. http://toomuchonherplate.com/stop-stress-eating-motivation-quotes/.

McGinnis, Patrick B. "Codependency-Abandonment of Self." Last modified October 12, 2009. http://www.dr-mcginnis.com/codependency.htm.

"Pema Chödrön Quotes." Goodreads. Accessed January 17, 2018. https://www.goodreads.com/quotes/593844-nothing-ever-goes-away-until-it-has-taught-us-what.

"Prevalence of child sexual abuse." Darkness To Light. http://www.d2l.org/the-issue/prevalence/.

Stibbs, John. "Emotional Boundaries in Relationships." Hidden Hurt. http://www.hiddenhurt.co.uk/emotional_boundaries.html.

Swaffer, Kate. "7 Cardinal Rules for Life." October 2, 2013. http://www.kateswaffer.com/2013/10/02/7-cardinal-rules-for-life/.

Tew, Robert. "As Long as You Are Breathing." Live Life Happy. June 28, 2013. https://livelifehappy.com/.

"To Be Strong Is to Experience Pain." *Positive Outlooks* (blog). January 14, 2014. https://positiveoutlooksblog.com/2014/01/14/to-experience-pain/.

U. of Alberta Sexual Assault Center. "What Is a Trigger?" Psych Central. https://psychcentral.com/lib/what-is-a-trigger/.

Vanzant, Iyanla. "Many of us have shame, guilt, pain, and anger attached to things we have done or experienced. We go to great lengths to hide what we have done or what has been done to us." Facebook, November 3, 2013. https://www.

facebook.com/DrIyanlaVanzant/photos/a.163309680368572.34873.150253431674197/660806407285561/?type=3&theater.

Wikipedia, s.v. "Personal Boundaries." Last modified January 7, 2018. https://en.m.wikipedia.org/wiki/Personal_boundaries.

Williamson, Marianne. *A Course in Weight Loss, 21 Spiritual Lessons for Surrendering Your Weight Forever*. Carlsbad: Hay House, 2010.

Williamson, Marianne. *Illuminata: A Return to Prayer*. London, UK: Penguin Books, 1994.

Zweig, Connie and Steve Wolf. *Romancing the Shadow*. Ballantine Books, 1997.

Appendix A

Helpful Resources

Alcoholics Anonymous (AA)—www.aa.org

Angela Dumas, a spiritual health coach—Angela@AngelaDumas.com

Beating Trauma, a blog by Elisabeth Corey—https://beatingtrauma.com

Darkness to Light Organization—www.d2l.org (End Child Sexual Abuse)

Emotional Freedom Techniques (EFT)—www.emofree.com or https://eft.mercola.com

isurvive.org—Resources on the home page list many types of help from hotlines to organizations and books for different countries. This is a private forum of survivors helping survivors, and it's heavily monitored for safety by volunteers. Excellent resource!

Overeaters Anonymous (OA)—www.oa.org

The Guest House Ocala, a trauma healing facility run by Judy Crane—www.theguesthouseocala.com/

Trauma Memory Information—www.kidspeace.org (how trauma memories are stored and how the brain is affected)

USA Crises Resources (as of May 2017)

- **Crisis Call Center for suicide prevention and crisis hotline**—http://www.crisiscallcenter.org/crisisservices.html
- **24/7 Crisis Support Call 775-784-8090** or **TEXT "ANSWER" to 839863**
- **24/7 Crisis Text Line**—TEXT "GO" to 741741
- **National Sexual Assault Hotline**—1-800-656-HOPE(4673) through the RAINN (Rape, Abuse & Incest National Network)
- **National Suicide Prevention Lifeline**—http://www.suicidepreventionlifeline.org to **CHAT** online or **CALL 1-800-273-TALK(8255)**
- **Safe Harbor 24/7 Emergency Hotline**—1-804-612-6126 in Richmond, Virginia, USA Safe Harbor empowers survivors of sexual and domestic violence to transform their lives and promote healthy relationships for all.
- **Teens Helping Teens**—teenlineonline.org
- CALL (800)-TLC-TEEN (852-8336) or TEXT "TEEN" to 839863 5:30 p.m.–9:30 p.m. PST

Additional Reading

Survivor Memoirs

There are many excellent survivor memoirs. I recommend reading different books because I have learned and gained so much strength from reading other survivors' stories. Here are some I've read that I recommend.

A Stolen Life: A Memoir by Jaycee Dugard

Deliver Us from Evil by Deborah Hunter-Marsh, MSW

Finding Me: A Decade of Darkness, A Life Reclaimed: A Memoir of the Cleveland Kidnappings by Michelle Knight with Michelle Buford

First Person Plural: My Life As a Multiple by Cameron West, PhD

It's OK to Tell: A Story of Hope and Recovery by Lauren Book

Nobody's Favorite: A Memoir by Victoria Stott

Prisoner of Another War: A Remarkable Journey of Healing From Childhood Trauma by Marilyn Murray

The Magic Daughter: A Memoir of Living with Multiple Personality Disorder by Jane Phillips

The Pink Elephant in the Middle of the Ghetto by TiTi Ladette

The River of Forgetting: A Memoir of Healing from Sexual Abuse by Jane Rowan

When Rabbit Howls by Truddi Chase

When You're Ready: A Woman's Healing from Childhood Physical and Sexual Abuse by Her Mother by Kathy Evert and Inie Bijkerk

Books for Educating Yourself about Trauma

Complex PTSD: From Surviving to Thriving by Pete Walker

In An Unspoken Voice: How the Body Releases Trauma and Restores Goodness by Peter A. Levine, PhD

The Betrayal Bond: Breaking Free of Exploitive Relationships by Patrick J. Carnes, PhD

Waking the Tiger: Healing Trauma by Peter A. Levine, PhD

The Body Keeps the Score: Brain, Mind, and Body in the Healing of Trauma by Bessel van der Kolk, MD

The Courage to Heal: A Guide for Women Survivors of Childhood Sexual Abuse by Ellen Bass and Lauren Davis

The Trauma Heart by Judy Crane

(Note: This is an excellent book for survivors and practitioners. It came out right before I sent this book for editing, and it's my favorite!)

Self-help and Educational

A Course in Weight Loss: 21 Spiritual Lessons for Surrendering Your Weight Forever by Marianne Williamson

Daring Greatly: How the Courage to Be Vulnerable Transforms the Way We Live, Love, Parent, and Lead by Brené Brown

(Note: Any books by Brené Brown—she works with shame)

Illuminata: A Return to Prayer by Marianne Williamson

Journey to the Heart: A 365-Day Guide to Thriving after Trauma by Svava Brooks

Love without Conditions: Reflections on the Christ Mind by Paul Ferrini

Radical Acceptance: Embracing Your Life with the Heart of a Buddha by Tara Brach, PhD

Releasing Your Authentic Self: A Daily Guide to Help Abuse and Trauma Survivors Rediscover Themselves by Svava Brooks

Appendix B

Self-Empowerment Coping Tools

The purpose of this section is to offer supportive coping tools to help when you're struggling and building strength. Notice which of these tools you gravitate toward. Try different tools and see which ones work for you. Then practice them. It's like building a muscle. You must practice using them and you'll get better at it.

Using coping tools can become second nature, and you'll prove to yourself that you're more powerful than any thought or emotion. These are worthwhile skills you take with you all your life, and they empower you to build your own helping toolbox and to move through life's challenges knowing you have effective ways to navigate life. You have the power to choose to assist yourself with supportive tools and prove to yourself that you will be all right, instead of using negative and self-destructive habits.

Many of the tools below were taught to me by my SHC (spiritual health coach), Angela Dumas.

Grounding/Centering/Calming Tools

Anxiety/Panic Self-soothing Tools

- Sit and focus your attention on your breath. Breathe deeply into your lower abdomen, in and out through your nose, thinking, *I'm only focusing on my breath, breathing in and breathing out. I'm calming down. I have the power within me to be peaceful.* You can tune into your body and identify where you're feeling a sensation. Once you find the sensation then focus your attention on it, breathe into it, and surround it with love. You can also ask yourself what your body is telling you but more importantly, see into your sensation with a curious mind. What am I seeing now? Breathe in, to the count of four, hold for four, and then breathe out to the count of eight. This will help activate your parasympathetic nervous system. That's the one that calms you on your out-breath.
- This may sound odd, but if you're panicking or really upset, you can force yourself to laugh like a lunatic. Laugh as hard as you can for at least a minute. It will knock your brain off the panic track and reset you. Then you can do your deep breathing.
- This one is a mind tool I've been practicing that helps me when I'm knocked off center or just ruminating. When I'm feeling a negative emotion and it's not trauma release work, I redirect myself the best I can to think of love. I like to think of how much I love God, and that makes me feel stronger and usually shifts my inner angst to a more peaceful state. You can focus on anything or anyone that you love—like your child or pet—to help you feel the presence of love within you. Being more

peaceful and not getting more upset (escalating anger, fear, or sadness) can positively affect whatever is going on in our world. Think about the far-reaching effects your peaceful behavior has. When we react with love, we defuse negativity, and the other person is more likely to act positively with others they are interacting with. This spreads through a domino effect from person to person: one act of loving-kindness affecting countless others.

- EFT (see Appendix A, Helpful Resources). There's an EFT (Emotional Freedom Technique) app too.
- Slowly expose yourself to triggers, see that you are okay, and you will extinguish them bit by bit. Remember, take baby steps!
- Visualize a very large scroll or white board and see your specific fear, thought, or just the name of the emotion you're experiencing written on it. You can write it or just see it written. Say, "I'm more than that. I'm bigger than that!" and watch it get erased because it's nothing. It's only a thought you are having, which is causing an emotion, which is making you feel bad. Emotion is nothing but an experience; it has no power other than what you give it by believing it is bigger and stronger than your mind. It's not! You have the power to choose, "Will I just be a floor mat and let my emotion control me, or will I use my tools to take control?"
- Visualize a calm grey energy swirling around at the center of your being—swirling very slowly while outside events whirl around you, not affecting you.
- Focus your attention on God or someone or something that you love dearly and connect with the feeling of love, talk yourself down. "I'm more than this. God/angels/the universe is helping

me right now. I only need to allow it." Connecting with love can shift any emotional state.

- Do ten big forced yawns in a row and then focus on your breath.
- If someone or something is triggering an intense emotional response in you, picture them as a small wind-up doll that has no power over you and laugh at it in your mind.
- Really get into dissecting your emotion by describing it in detail and breathing through it. For example:
    - Anxiety. I'm anxious; I feel my throat constricting; I'm scared; my breathing is shallow; my whole body is tense; I want to hide.
    - Anger: I'm raging; I want to scream; I want to crush something; my body feels tight; I'm clenching my teeth.

By describing it in detail, focusing on tuning into yourself, and honoring where you're at, it can de-escalate your emotional state. Remember to breathe deeply, as your breathing tells your mind to physiologically calm down.

- This one is an exercise in acceptance. Ask yourself or have someone else ask you the following questions:
    - *Can I say yes to my fear and approve of me anyway and give myself love because I'm the master of my being?*
    - Can I allow myself to feel fear and still love me?
    - Can I just let myself be who I am right now, a person experiencing fear and still love me?
    - *Where am I feeling fear in my body? What's it telling me?*

Once you identify it, surround it in a loving light, comfort it, and tell it that it's okay to be with you now. "I let my fear be as it is and then it will just change. I accept me and my feelings. I deserve to be loved and accepted unconditionally, no matter what. I approve of all of me without trying to change. I'm allowed to feel my fear. Can I say yes to me and my fear and love myself anyway?"

- Look in the mirror for a few minutes daily and tell yourself you love yourself with loving eyes. Keep going even when you are thinking, *Yeah right!* Just keep going, and you'll eventually experience a shift toward love.
- Ask yourself what's the most loving and comforting thing you could do for yourself right now or today. Make sure you pick realistic things and follow through. Some ideas are: taking a nap, having a bath, reading, walking outside, or making yourself a cup of tea.

Boundary/Protection Tools

- Create your own safe house/place in your mind to go or invite your current and/or younger parts to go when you're scared or need comforting. You can visualize a hut filled with stuffed animals and pillows or whatever feels safe to you.
- Imagine yourself in an army tank or in knight's armor.
- Use the "Shields Up" saying or make up your own to remind yourself to protect yourself (you can imagine a shield around you or imagine you're in a golden bubble of protection) while you are exposed to something that is stressing or triggering you. Your shield doesn't allow anyone else's toxic or intense energy near you.

Empowerment Tools

- Find quotes that you identify with and that give you strength; repeat them often.
- Acknowledge your strengths and all the creative ways your child and adult selves survived, whether they're considered positive or negative.
- Find your voice (work on opening your throat chakra with an energy healer/shaman/on your own with a book or DVD) and speak up for yourself (start small and work your way up to bigger things).
- Visualize yourself as a giant who is towering over a very tiny Earth. You see what you're afraid of—a thought or emotion—as a speck on the ground. You bend way down and pick up that speck and crush it in between your index and thumb and then fling it out into the universe. You have the power; you only need to believe that truth.

Grounding in the Present Moment Tools

- Stomp your feet and remind yourself of your age, where you are, the fact that you're an adult now, and that you have the power to stay in the present moment.
- Take a cold bath or shower for twenty minutes, or as long as you can tolerate it. This will shock you onto another track. This is for more extreme states when you're desperate.
- Walk outside and notice what's around you in the moment.
- Chant the root chakra sound LAM pronounced "LNG." You can hear it on YouTube. This chakra is your grounding

connection to the center of the Earth, and it's located at your perineum. While chanting, visualize a root coming from both your feet, down to the center of the Earth, and connecting to a crystal at Earth's center. Hopefully, you will feel a more solid connection to the present moment.

Inner Child and Integration Tools

- Acknowledge your younger parts. Communicate with them, visualize them in your mind, and accept, comfort, and protect them. Go at their pace and give them a chance to build trust. They have been traumatized, and their basic trust is broken, so go easy.
- Imagine your AS carrying your younger self in a sling, sitting in your lap, or just sitting with them while they play or rest or cry, etc.
- Have ICW (Inner Child Work) conversations in which you ask how they are, how can you help them, do they want to play, etc. Does your child self want to tell you what happened to him or her?
- Play (color/paint/dolls/movie/hike/video gaming, etc.) and check in and see how your younger self is doing.
- Offer a re-do, where your AS comforts/protects/nurtures your younger self during painful times in your past.
- Be your inner child's witness to their memories, emotions, or whatever they need to express, as long as you hold safe boundaries for yourself.

Self-expression Tools

Express whatever you're going through in an uncensored manner by painting/journaling/drawing/dancing/doing yoga or some other type of movement. You can also sing/scream/cook/play an instrument/sculpt/say what you always wanted to say to someone by role playing in your mind and speaking out loud. Write your story! Do whatever you need to do, just get that rage/grief/shame/guilt/terror out and make more room for positives to move in. See what you gravitate to because that's your inner healer guiding you. Check in with yourself to determine if you're gravitating to an old unhealthy way of coping. Make sure the activity is strengthening and supportive.

Spiritually Centering Tools

- Meditate. Focus on deep abdominal breaths, or do a slow walking meditation and focus on taking each next step on the ground.
- Form your own forgiveness practice. Every time a self-defeating and judging thought comes up in your mind that you know weakens you, think, *I love and forgive myself for everything. All the things I've judged as being my fault or not my fault. I love and accept myself no matter what—no exceptions and no conditions.* Those victim thoughts and other negative thoughts are, on a very deep level, a call for love and support. They come from a damaged part of yourself, so the most effective response is to give yourself loving acceptance and support.
- Ask God/angels/the universe to help you focus on love. Spend a few minutes to do this periodically throughout the day or even once a day—remember, what you focus on grows.

There's a theme running through these tools: Change your focus and believe in your power to choose how you respond to what you perceive. In short, it's self-empowerment. Remember: what you focus on is what will grow, so step out of the problem and put your attention toward a solution.

Appendix C

A Note from My Child and Adult Selves on Child Abuse Education

I promised Little Marie that I would include this note to you, along with child abuse education, statistics, information on secrets, and why children don't tell.

A note from Little Marie: I want more parents to be careful and watch their children more closely. Please don't blindly trust anyone with your children. Please don't let your child go anywhere alone. Don't let them be alone with other adults, and pay attention to how your child acts. We'll usually *show* you something is wrong by changing how we act and having problems with our bodies, like stomach aches and pain, or trouble at school, but *not* by telling you with words what we are so scared and embarrassed of.

A note from my AS on children still suffering: It's extremely important to shine a light on all the children still suffering at the hands of abusers. The reality is that children are being sexually assaulted every day, and this needs to be dealt with. The statistics as of writing this are as follows:

"Research shows that one in 10 children will be the victim of sexual abuse before their 18th birthday."[39] Sadly, in 2015, 400,000 babies born are estimated to be sexually abused.[40] Those are just the reported statistics! This is an epidemic, and not talking about it isn't going to help the child whose only hope is an aware adult that is willing to listen and take action on their behalf.

My hope is for more adults to be willing to look at this painful reality and become more aware. Let's help every child we can who is suffering at the hands of an abuser or about to have their world as they know it come crashing down. Then we can help prevent child abuse one child at a time and help identify children who have been abused and need help with healing. Helping child survivors heal would result in a lot fewer wounded adults engaging in addictions and other self-destructive behaviors that can ruin their own lives and the lives of their loved ones.

Every case of child sexual abuse has profound consequences for that child but also for our society. The trauma will manifest in one form or another, such as paying for child or adult survivors' psychological and addiction hospitalizations or other treatment, or having the survivors' children being awarded to the state because their parent can't function. Any way you look at it, so many people pay for the horrific act of an adult abusing a child. Do you know there are pedophiles that have abused hundreds of children in one lifetime? The more we know, the more we are aware, the more we can prevent childhood sexual abuse together as a united force.

---

39 "Prevalence of child sexual abuse," Darkness to Light, http://www.d2l.org/the-issue/prevalence/, 2013.

40 "Prevalence of child sexual abuse," Darkness to Light.

* * *

The following note is for anyone who may know of a child being molested. If someone knows of or has witnessed a child being abused and hasn't called the police—not just their supervisor or board of directors (e.g., Penn State) but the police—they are playing a part in that child's abuse. Whatever or whomever they think they are protecting at that child's expense is meaningless compared to the hell the child will live through their *whole life*! There are no excuses, no exceptions, and no justifications for standing by and allowing that child to go through more devastation that will torment them indefinitely. Help that child out of their living hell and protect another child, because there will be more children assaulted by that pedophile. There should be no question about whether to call the police. You can make an anonymous call. It will come out eventually, and those who knew and did nothing will suffer in the personal prison cell of their mind, knowing they did nothing to help a child in desperate need.

As adult survivors of sexual abuse, we need to be extra vigilant with our children because abuse has a tendency to repeat through generations. This does not mean that adult survivors abuse children! It can be someone in the family or outside the family abusing the adult survivor's child. Please don't be an oblivious parent. Watch your children closely; observe your child's unspoken body language and listen to your gut. Children will tell you in some way that something is wrong.

If you have an inkling or know your child is being abused and haven't called the police, call them now. The pain and guilt you and your child will live with all your lives will be far worse than your fears of losing your home or whatever you think you're protecting by not calling the police. If you don't protect your children now, they will grow up with many disruptive behaviors and hatred toward you; both of you will be tormented by that. By saving your child, you are also saving yourself. You can make it through with support, and there are organizations that will help you (see Appendix A, Helpful Resources).

* * *

If you're a survivor of childhood trauma, then you know about holding secrets. Secrets give abusers power to keep abusing. A very important reason is that *secrets allow hidden sexual assaults to continue, and those secrets protect the abusers and imprison the victim in torment.* I talk about my abuse now, but when I was little, the men who raped me depended on me not saying a word.

As a survivor of childhood sexual assault, I'm asking you to help shine a light on it, talk about it, and offer support. We can help abused children and each other. As survivors, we don't have the luxury of being oblivious to the suffering of others because we live with the painful reality of our own abuse. It's time to rip the dark blanket of secrecy from this societal atrocity and to speak of it out loud, even though it's uncomfortable for people to hear.

Why Children Don't Tell

Having a fuller knowledge of this subject has helped me with navigating my own experiences, and I hope it will help you too. I just couldn't wrap my head around why I couldn't remember and why I couldn't tell. I combined what I know from my own experience with information from an excellent organization called Darkness to Light.[41] It's an organization working to prevent childhood sexual abuse by advocating and educating. Their site explains how abusers shame children into thinking the abuse is the child's fault or that their parents will get angry. Some abusers confuse children by presenting the abuse as a game and manipulating them to play. They may do special loving things with the child prior to abusing them to gain trust and form an attachment. This behavior is called *grooming*. Many abusers also use the tactic of threatening children and their family or pet.

Abusers try to convince the child that the abuse feels good in order to add to the child's shame and try to confuse them so they won't tell. The abuser may think the child is so young that they won't know what they're doing or remember it. As was true for me at age four, very young children just don't understand what's happening to them.

Pedophiles are careful to keep injuries to a minimum so they are hidden or less noticeable to the adults in the child's life. The pedophiles rely on the child's passivity and the abuser's threats to keep the abuse a secret. Many abusers are authority figures who have an established trust relationship with the child. As a result, the child may sense that the interaction between them does not feel right, but the abuser's authority position and the child's fears compel them to override those feelings and comply with the abuser. There are also the pedophiles that see an opportunity and just attack.

As a side note here, when a person's sexuality is tapped at a young age by abuse and then later on as an adult when they encounter sexual

---

41 Darkness to Light, http://www.d2l.org.

advances, they may automatically go into a compliant response or immobility state (when a trauma trigger causes them to not be able to move) because that is how they survived in the past. This is because their early sexual associations got imprinted on their brains and cause a dissociated response. It appears they are consenting, when in fact they're not.

Finally, here is another reason children don't tell. A particularly shameful and painful belief for many survivors of sexual abuse is that if their body responded to sexual stimulation, they believe some awful part of them must have liked it. This is yet another cruel lie the traumatized mind unknowingly tells itself. The human body's sexual organs were made to respond, and they will respond in many cases regardless of how repulsive the victim's mind knows their abuse to be. But many survivors don't know this, so they condemn themselves of a crime they didn't commit. Survivors, just because your body did what it was made to do, it in no way means you wanted to be abused or enjoyed it. Please let yourself off the hook with that false belief. Childhood sexual abuse (CSA) is PROFOUNDLY CONFUSING for child and adult survivors.

The list of reasons children don't tell goes on and on. It's all so confusing; a minefield of complexities that a child doesn't know how to navigate safely. Let's not forget the situations when children just can't remember because the memory is too scary.

Signs and Symptoms of Abuse

The Darkness to Light website points out physical symptoms to look for, such as rashes, bruises, redness, swelling in the genital area, and urinary tract infections. More red flags should go up when you observe the child who is anxious and/or has frequent stomach aches and headaches. Watch for the child who acts too emotionally or behaviorally perfect. They may be overcompensating for feeling bad inside and trying just a little too hard.

Attention issues like ADD and learning disabilities are something to take note of. Recall that I had been diagnosed with ADD, dyslexia, and auditory processing issues. It also could have been a brain altered by trauma. The developing brain has areas that get more attention and oxygen during their development at different stages. The traumatized, hypervigilant child's brain can form differently by sending more energy to the fight-or-flight related areas, thus depriving other developing areas of needed energy to develop. This could result in the underdeveloped areas experiencing learning deficits and attention issues, among other things.

Behaviors such as anger, withdrawal, depression, unexplained rebellion, or acting out sexually should be noted; sudden changes in behavior should be checked into immediately. The suspicious observer needs to put the behavioral, physical, and psychological puzzle pieces together, along with their gut feelings, when trying to determine if a child may be at risk of being abused. Supposedly, there may be no signs, but I question that idea.

Another reason to be suspicious is when an animal is being abused in a household. It's a major red flag that abuse is happening elsewhere in that home. The abuser starts with the most vulnerable, a pet, and works their way up to vulnerable family members. The abuser's violent behavior can eventually escalate to strangers. Where there is one type of abuse, you will usually find others—sexual, emotional, and physical abuse—all happening to the same victims under one roof. It's just heartbreaking!

In Closing

Children are more open and sensitive, and their wounds go deep. Those old myths or beliefs that kids are so resilient that they can just get over horrible things is a lie. Yes, we are strong enough to go on and live through our horrors, but we live with so much fallout! That "getting over it" belief is there to comfort adults' guilt and give those involved an excuse to do nothing to help. Taking action, like talking openly and honestly, providing therapy, encouraging creative expression, and offering a supportive spiritual belief system are some ways to help a child heal. Dealing with the truth helps a child, but sweeping it under the carpet, blaming the child, and holding secrets, just condemns them to a prison of pain.

Lastly, when youths realize their looks or provocative behavior have power to get them attention and they experiment with it by flirting, they don't think about where it can lead because they are learning about being a girl or a boy, and about relationships in general. They are naturally interested in exploring those relationships. They want to get attention and to socialize. It doesn't occur to them that some sick person is going to attack them and commit a crime. Their natural behavior doesn't warrant rape. If I want to flirt and wear tight pants, I should have the right to make that choice of self-expression without worrying about being attacked. And anyone who chooses to rape another for any reason is a criminal, so let's stop pointing out what the victim was wearing and instead talk about the violent choices the perpetrator made.

Appendix D

Trauma Education and Triggers

I decided to include this appendix because understanding different aspects of trauma and trauma triggers can be challenging. I found trauma education to be supportive in helping me gain a deeper understanding of what complex trauma is, which in turn assisted me with being more patient with myself and my healing process. I hope this information is helpful to you too.

PTSD

Post-traumatic stress disorder (PTSD) is a debilitating condition that follows a terrifying event. Often, people with PTSD have persistent frightening thoughts and memories of their ordeal and feel emotionally numb, especially with people they were once close to. PTSD, once referred to as shell shock or battle fatigue, was first brought to public attention by war veterans, but it can result from any number of traumatic incidents. These include kidnapping; surgery; serious accidents, such as car or train wrecks; natural disasters, such as floods or earthquakes; violent attacks, such as mugging, rape, or torture; or being held captive. The event that triggers it may be something that threatened the person's life or the life of someone close to him or her. Or it could be something witnessed, such as mass destruction after a plane crash.

Whatever the source of the problem, some people with PTSD repeatedly relive the trauma in the form of nightmares and disturbing recollections during the day. They may also experience sleep problems, depression, feeling detached or numb, or being easily startled. They may lose interest in things they used to enjoy and have trouble feeling affectionate. They may feel irritable, more aggressive, or even violent. Seeing things that remind them of the incident may be very distressing, which could lead them to avoid certain places or situations that bring back those memories. Anniversaries of the event are often very difficult.

PTSD can occur at any age, including childhood. The disorder can be accompanied by depression, substance abuse, or anxiety. Symptoms may be mild or severe—people may become easily irritated or have violent outbursts. In severe cases they may have trouble working or socializing. In general, the symptoms seem to be worse if the event that traumatized them was initiated by a person, also called interpersonal violence, such as a rape, as opposed to a flood.

Ordinary events can serve as reminders of the trauma and trigger flashbacks or intrusive images. A flashback may make the person lose touch with reality and reenact the event for a period of seconds or hours or, very rarely, days. A person having a flashback, which can come in the form of images, sounds, smells, or feelings, usually believes that the traumatic event is happening all over again.

Not every traumatized person gets full-blown PTSD or experiences PTSD at all. PTSD is diagnosed only if the symptoms last more than a month. In those who do have PTSD, symptoms usually begin within three months of the trauma, and the course of the illness varies. Some people recover within six months, while others have symptoms that last much longer. In some cases, the condition may be chronic. Occasionally, the illness doesn't show up until years after the traumatic event.[42]

I want to mention once again how trauma insidiously affects one's behavior and emotional state, regardless of the amount of time that has passed. So, whether it has been one day, or forty years, significant symptoms and self-medication can be present. The idea that someone should just "get over it" is not only passé but wrong, and as a society, we need to let that belief system go and embrace the need for survivors to heal.

To learn more about PTSD, visit www.psychcentral.com

The Trauma Brain

The amygdala is a primitive or reptilian part of the brain where traumatic memories get stored, and it has no concept of time. The amygdala stores fear and aggression memories and plays a role in how emotions are expressed. Trauma memories are stored totally different from normal nontraumatic memories. The old trauma becoming confused with current experiences stems from trauma memories involuntarily getting triggered and coming up to the surface along with any current distress.

All traumas come up at once, since the amygdala does not have a space and time reference, like the brain's rational cerebral cortex does. Rather, these are involuntary responses or symptoms being

42 John Grohol, "Post-Traumatic Stress Disorder, Introduction to PTSD Symptoms & Treatment," Psych Central, https://psychcentral.com/disorders/ptsd/.

driven by the reptilian brain, which is instinctively geared for survival. This experience is confusing because it's in the form of emotional and physical responses. For example, there may be feelings of being overwhelmed when the circumstances may not fit feeling overwhelmed; dissociation (feeling disoriented and detached); fight or flight (both include trembling, shaking, increased heart rate, sweating, etc.); and freeze/immobility (feeling like you can't move).

Many times, the primitive trauma response occurs without the picture memories of the old events, so it appears to be a mystery. The person experiencing all of this then asks, "Why am I such a mess? This situation is bad, but not bad enough to put me over the top. Yet I feel over the top." And then, many of us turn on ourselves at this point and ask, "What is wrong with me?" and "Why am I so weak?" etc.

In summary, the amygdala doesn't distinguish between what happened then and what is happening now, because there is no time involved. This reptilian part of the brain isn't like the cerebral cortex region that has executive functions for relating experience to time and being able to rationalize with it. You can't rationalize with the amygdala, but you can use the higher-order thinking of the cerebral cortex to navigate your way out of trigger responses (amygdala responses). So, as you move through your healing process of remembering, releasing, and getting help, you are moving your trauma from your amygdala to your cerebral cortex, where you can better cope using awareness and healing tools to manage your responses and calm yourself down.

Note: I focus here on the amygdala, but the brain's limbic system and hippocampus are involved with trauma memories too. Also, the amygdala and hippocampus may have lesions and be stunted in growth as a result of childhood trauma.

This damage to the brain may be seen on ECT scans. Another reason to treat trauma is that trauma actually changes the brain's physiology, causing these lesions. *In other words, just ignoring it or trying to push it away won't help you.* The effects of trauma on the brain don't just disappear over time.

Triggers

A *trigger* is something that sets off a memory tape or flashback, transporting the person back to the event of her or his original trauma.

Triggers are very personal; different things trigger different people. The survivor may begin to avoid situations and stimuli that he or she thinks triggered the flashback. He or she will react to this flashback or trigger with an emotional intensity similar to that at the time of the trauma event. A person's triggers are activated through one or more of the five senses: sight, sound, touch, smell, and taste. For more on triggers, visit https://psychcentral.com/lib/what-is-a-trigger/.

Appendix E

List of Acronyms and Glossary of Terms

Acronyms

ADD – attention-deficit disorder

ADS – adolescent self

AD – adult self

CSA – child sexual abuse

CS – child self

C-PTSD – complex posttraumatic stress disorder

EFT – Emotional Freedom Technique

ICW – inner child work

PTSD – posttraumatic stress disorder

SAC – sexual assault counselor

SHC – spiritual health coach

Glossary of Terms

> **Note:** The repressed memories I speak of throughout my book are formally referred to as *trauma-induced amnesia* or *repressed memory syndrome*. They are described later in this section.

Body Memories – Since trauma is also stored at the cellular level, survivors have memories that come up by experiencing physical symptoms, such as headaches, gastro symptoms, pain, the body waking up at a recurring time, tingling sensations, etc. The symptoms can be expressed in many ways but have some symbolic connection to the original abuse or traumatic event. The body is an ally and will tell a person what they need to know if the person is willing to listen. It's like the body is a guide, sounding the alarm and asking the survivor to pay attention because there are wounds that need to be addressed and cared for.

Boundaries – I'll mention three definitions here since boundaries are such an important concept to understand and be aware of, especially for survivors of sexual abuse. **1)** Personal boundaries are guidelines, rules, or limits that a person creates to identify for themselves what are reasonable ways for other people to behave around him or her and how they will respond when someone steps outside those limits. They are built from a mix of beliefs, opinions, attitudes, past experiences, and social learning.[43] **2)** Regions separating two psychological or social systems. A central concept in Systems Theory pertaining

43 Wikipedia, s.v. "Personal Boundaries," last modified January 7, 2018, https://en.m.wikipedia.org/wiki/Personal_boundaries.

to the implicit rules that determine how the family members or subsystems are expected to relate to one another and to nonfamily members. Healthy family functioning largely entails clear boundaries; less healthy functioning is seen where boundary subsystems are either inappropriately rigid or not consistently clear (i.e., in a *disengaged family* or an *enmeshed family*).[44] **3)** Personal adult boundaries are the limits we set in relationships that allow us to protect ourselves from being manipulated by, or enmeshed with, emotionally needy others. Such boundaries come from having a good sense of our own self-worth.[45]

Codependency – I've read many definitions and settled with this website's description of codependency. McGinnis explains that codependency applies "to just about anyone who has a pattern of dysfunctional relationships involving focusing on the needs and behaviors of others more than one's own. Codependent individuals become so preoccupied and focused on the needs of others that they neglect their own needs. Two key areas in a person's life reflect codependence: the relationship with the self and relationships with others." Codependency "is a treatable progressive disorder with common symptoms. Some symptoms are: low self-esteem, caretaking, obsession, dependency on others to meet needs and wants, difficulty expressing anger appropriately, having weak boundaries, anxiety, depression, … perfectionism, operating in extremes …." He goes on to explain how codependency originates in the family of origin that struggles with addictions, abuse, and mental illness. "Shaming, abandonment, and neglect flourish in these families." Lastly, "fear of being your authentic self, resulting in power patterns (controlling or

---

44 Robert L. Barker, *Social Work Dictionary*, 5th ed. (NASW, 2003), 49.

45 John Stibbs, "Emotional Boundaries in Relationships," Hidden Hurt, http://www.hiddenhurt.co.uk/emotional_boundaries.html.

compliance to manipulate) to get what you believe you can't ask or demand from others. Codependents fear abandonment and rejection. In giving up their authentic selves they perform the ultimate abandonment—that of oneself."[46]

Complex-PTSD or C-PTSD – This is a form of PTSD that originates from trauma that occurred over a prolonged period of time in childhood. Its core characteristics are psychological fragmentation or compartmentalized memories; loss of a coherent sense of self (awareness of others but not so much of self); loss of a sense of safety, trust, and self-worth; and a tendency to be re-victimized. There can also be difficulty regulating emotions, explosive rage, forgetting traumatic events (repression), and feeling detached from mental processes and the body. In addition, one can be unable to feel one's own emotions and be persistently anxious and in a hyper-aroused state that leads to anger and addiction issues and/or engaging in risky behaviors.

Crisis Phase – The book *Courage to Heal* calls this the Emergency Stage. This is a period of time when a person's abuse comes to the forefront of their mind and becomes all they can think about in an obsessive way. When the survivor is remembering for the first time since their abuse, it can be intense and brutal to withstand. "You may find yourself talking about it obsessively with anyone who will listen. Your life may become full of practical crises which totally overwhelm you. You may find yourself having flashbacks uncontrollably, crying all day long, or unable to go to work. You may dream about your abuser and be unable to sleep .... The important thing to remember

46 Patrick B. McGinnis, "Codependency-Abandonment of Self," last modified October 12, 2009, http://www.dr-mcginnis.com/codependency.htm.

is that the emergency stage is a natural part of the healing process and will come to an end.... There will be a time when you will not think, eat, and dream sexual abuse twenty-four hours a day."[47]

Defense Mechanisms – "Defense mechanisms are one way of looking at how people distance themselves from a full awareness of unpleasant thoughts, feelings and behaviors.... Most defense mechanisms are fairly unconscious—that means most of us don't realize we're using them in the moment."[48] Through self-awareness work, such as therapy, the defense mechanisms become conscious. The following are some of the defense mechanisms I've mentioned in my story, but there are many more that are not listed here:

Compartmentalizing – "... is a lesser form of dissociation, wherein parts of oneself are separated from awareness of other parts ..."[49] Compartmentalizing is a primitive defense mechanism whereby a person disconnects thoughts and feelings that appear dangerous to their well-being from other parts of themselves. Children tend to automatically use the more primitive defenses, and this can get carried on into adulthood. This process of disconnecting makes the person have a lot of thoughts and feelings in separate compartments that don't communicate with each other.

Conversion – Converting anxiety or internal conflict into a physical symptom, such as paralysis or pain.

---

47 Bass and Davis, *The Courage to Heal*, 72–75.

48 John Grohol, "15 Common Defense Mechanisms," https://psychcentral.com/lib/15-common-defense-mechanisms/.

49 Grohol, "15 Common Defense Mechanisms."

Denial – Unconsciously blocking anything that's too difficult to consciously hold.

Dissociation – Disconnecting from oneself to avoid being emotionally and physically overwhelmed by traumatic stress. For example, when a person looks zoned out after a traumatic event and can't remember what happened. It's a form of disconnecting oneself from horrible events, thoughts, and feelings in order to survive. This is how Patti described it: the pathological dissociation piece is the feeling of being in a daze, on auto-pilot (robotic), or in a dream, and being unable to control your body with an emotional and cognitive overload sensation.

Intellectualizing – Intellectualization is when someone focuses on thinking when confronted with an unacceptable impulse, situation, or behavior without allowing any emotions because the emotion is intolerable.

Repression – "Repression is the unconscious blocking of unacceptable thoughts, feelings, and impulses. The key to repression is that people do it unconsciously, so they often have little control over it. "Repressed memories" are memories that have been unconsciously blocked from access or view."[50] Repressed memories are called repressed memory syndrome and trauma-induced amnesia.

The world of a trauma survivor can be a very intense place, especially when the trauma was severe enough to cause full repression of the event(s). I don't mean a light forgetting where memories can be retrieved with some effort. I mean the memories

50 Grohol, "15 Common Defense Mechanisms."

that are consciously irretrievable even with a lot of effort to get at them. That level of repression is the mind's way of protecting the survivor. But if left there indefinitely, the repressed memories become destructive.

EMDR – The therapeutic use of specific eye movements to reprocess traumatic memories. It was developed by Francine Shapiro and uses bilateral stimulation of the left and right sides of the brain to re-process trauma for healing.

Exposure Therapy – Exposure therapy is a specific type of cognitive-behavioral psychotherapy technique that's often used in the treatment of posttraumatic stress disorder (PTSD) and phobias. It's when you slowly expose yourself to an anxiety-provoking situation and see that you are okay. The slow exposure to a panic trigger lessens the panic or fear by desensitizing you over time. It's a good idea to do exposure therapy with a trained professional, especially if you're new to it, and it needs to be accompanied with learning relaxation and mindfulness techniques first. I recommend considering other therapies, such as EMDR and Somatic Experiencing that have less of a probability of causing secondary trauma.

Flashbacks – A flashback, or involuntary recurrent memory, is a psychological phenomenon in which an individual has a sudden, usually powerful, re-experiencing of a past experience or elements of a past experience.

Grounding Techniques – Grounding is a technique that helps keep someone in the present moment. It helps reorient a person to the here-and-now, to reality. Grounding skills can be helpful in managing overwhelming feelings or intense anxiety. They help someone to regain their mental focus from an often intensely emotional state. Some examples that help one ground in the present moment are walking outside, being in nature in general, and stomping your feet and affirming your current age, name, location, etc.

Inner Child Work (ICW) – A process of connecting with the child within that was wounded and is stuck at certain developmental stages. This work entails the adult self communicating with and allowing their young wounded self to express themselves with their older self, who represents a safe person. The adult self earns the inner child's trust and parents the younger self with love and protection, which, in turn, helps the inner child heal over time. Here are two links for additional information on ICW:

https://healthpsychologyconsultancy.wordpress.com/2012/04/21/who-is-your-inner-child/

https://www.psychologytoday.com/blog/evil-deeds/200806/essential-secrets-psychotherapy-the-inner-child

Posttraumatic Stress Disorder (PTSD) – See C-PTSD and Appendix A for a description.

Psychological Transference – An experience where feelings and perceptions you had for someone when you were a child, such as a parent, got transferred to someone in your current life, which blocks your ability to see the current person as they actually are.

The Shadow – Describes the part of the psyche that an individual would rather not acknowledge. It contains the denied parts of self that surface in one way or another. Bringing Shadow material into consciousness drains its dark power, and one can even recover valuable resources from it. When you accept your shadow parts and integrate them as acceptable and valuable components of yourself, you will realize hidden gifts and make great strides forward in your personal growth.

Somatic Experiencing – A therapy used for trauma recovery that utilizes the body's sensations and empowering memories to work through the client's trauma. Peter Levine developed Somatic Experiencing.

Trauma-Focused Cognitive Behavior Therapy or TF-CBT – This treatment approach entails working with trauma education, mood regulation, and gradual exposure to triggers, as well as cognitive distortions (e.g., victims believing it was their fault and that they are damaged and worthless). TF-CBT treatment can address the C-PTSD pieces that deal with three fundamental areas: emotional dysregulation, pathological dissociation, and stress-related breakdowns like with bodily health.

Trauma-Induced Amnesia or Repressed Memory Syndrome – Trauma-induced amnesia and repressed memory syndrome appear to occur from excessive stress, fear, and arousal overwhelming the primitive survival part of the brain called the hippocampus. In other words, trauma changes your brain structure by shrinking the hippocampus portion of the brain and affecting your brain's neuro-chemical functionality. Trauma memories can totally disappear until triggered, which can be many years later. When they reappear, they are usually fragmented and have a different quality about them when compared with memories that were stored normally.

Trauma Triggers – A trauma trigger is something that sets off a memory tape or flashback, transporting the person back to the event of his/her original trauma. A person's triggers are activated through one or more of the five senses: sight, sound, touch, smell, and taste.[51] Thinking or talking about abuse or strong negative emotions can also be a trigger.

51 U. of Alberta Sexual Assault Center, "What is a Trigger?" Psych Central, https://psychcentral.com/lib/what-is-a-trigger/.

About the Author

Repeated childhood sexual traumas created an insidious array of symptoms and struggles that held Marie down. There were days when she couldn't get out of bed and times when she felt unfit to be around others. Her belief was that she would be a victim for a lifetime.

Marie shares a depth of insight into healing from childhood trauma, from 25 years of engaging in her own healing, studying trauma for over a decade, and practicing as a trauma psychotherapist. She's now thriving after years of suffering from her childhood pain and hopes you'll join her and stand together as survivors while learning how she obtained the gift of PEACE. You too can learn more about releasing yourself from your pain by reading her book that shows you how she walked through her pain into well-being.

You can connect with Marie on social media or her website where she'll offer you a free coping skills checklist for comfort, stabilizing yourself and more, along with a helpful guided meditation.